THE DARK SECRETS OF MANIPULATION AND MIND CONTROL

LEARN HOW TO SPOT MANIPULATION, BRAINWASHING, MIND CONTROL, AND DECEPTION TECHNIQUES AND TURN THEM TO YOUR ADVANTAGE IN EVERYDAY LIFE.

Table of Contents

Introduction

WHAT IS MANIPULATION?

Manipulation is defined as the "control or influence over a situation or person in a way that is done unfairly, very cleverly, and unscrupulously". Now, the term manipulation gets thrown around a lot, but the correct way to define manipulation is when you try to play upon or control a person or situation by resorting to artful, insidious, or unfair means; especially if this is done for your advantage. As Merriam-Webster defines it, manipulation means "To control or play upon others by means which are unfair or insidious, especially for their own advantage and to serve their own purpose."

Manipulation is a deceptive art, and those who have mastered this art form are referred to as manipulators. Manipulative individuals exist everywhere and it includes that person who only gets in touch with you when they want or need something. Or that coworker who only strikes up a conversation or compliments you when they need a "favor" from you but doesn't bother to keep in touch once you've helped them out. Manipulators make it seem like their behavior is no big deal and it's a part of "who they are". They can smile, charm, compliment you and tell you what you want to hear but make no mistake about it, they are extremely dangerous individuals.

The worst part is that it's hard to identify who might be a manipulator immediately because on the surface, they make you believe that they're amazing. They make you yearn to be part of their clique. They make you believe that they love you. They are charming, persuasive, and might even go to great lengths to forge some kind relationship with you. However, underneath all that lies a sinister, underhanded character that has been toying with your emotions all along. Beneath that smiling exterior hides a personality who will not hesitate to stab you in the back the first chance they get if it means they get to reap all the benefits from it.

The problem with manipulators is that they don't consider their behavior to be destructive at all. They have convinced themselves that their needs are so important that it doesn't matter what they do so far as it results in them getting their way. They believe the end justifies the means and it doesn't matter if they have to backstab, throw people under the bus or step on several toes to get what they want.

Unfortunately, if you're a manipulator, then you're a bully. What is even more unfortunate about the whole situation is the fact that the world we live in is full of these types of individuals. People who will stop at nothing, who will do, say, and go to any lengths to get what they want, even at the expense of others. We see them every day all around us. That co-worker who withholds useful information from you, so that they can get ahead of you. People who would rather record an incident of someone in distress on their mobile phones, to share on social media, than step in to help because "they don't want to get involved". Those who have no qualms about using you for their personal gain. People who love watching and instigating drama so that it deflects the attention away from them, while they revel in the misery of others. Manipulators are everywhere, and they don't think about how anyone else feels because they're far too concerned about their own selfish needs. They don't care about the consequences of their actions as long as they get what they want, and they certainly don't care enough about you to be concerned over your feelings.

MANIPULATION VS. PERSUASION

Many people fail to recognize the nuances between manipulation and persuasion. Although both seek to convince an individual to do something they wouldn't have done in the first place, the two are quite different; enough to be regarded as completely separate concepts. Manipulation is only beneficial to the manipulator while persuasion, on the other hand, usually benefits both parties involved. The manipulator sees the other person as a tool and a means to an end, whereas the persuader sees the other person as a partner. In essence, due to these key differences, manipulation is far more insidious than persuasion.

Defining Persuasion

Although persuasion involves changing the mind of someone else, it is not necessarily a bad thing as there are plenty of ways that persuasion can be used innocently or benevolently. Therefore, persuasion is any method that will actively change the thoughts, emotions, actions, or attitudes of another person toward another person or thing. This change is regarded as persuasion and it can be done inwardly toward oneself through changing one's attitude, or it can be done to other people as well.

Usually, persuasion is used as a form of influence and it is everywhere. It is present in ads, politics, schools, professions, and just about everywhere you could think of. If you can think of something, chances are there is some sort of persuasive layer to it somewhere and somehow.

When persuading someone, four key elements must be present. They are:

- The individual doing the persuading.
- The intended message.
- A target recipient for the persuasion.
- The context in which persuasion is received.

Each of these four key elements must be present for something to be considered persuasive. Of course, this means that manipulation would fall within the category of persuasion as well.

Defining Manipulation

In psychology, manipulation is a type of influence or persuasion, but unlike regular persuasion, manipulation is covert, deceptive, or underhanded. This means that, unlike regular persuasion, which seeks to be most honest, manipulation is often untrustworthy. The manipulator will have no qualms about lying about the situation or attempting to coerce the target into believing something, so long as he gets what he wants.

The manipulator only seeks to serve himself; he does not care that his decisions might affect the other party negatively. The target is seen as little more than collateral damage, a necessary sacrifice to get the desired results. As a result, manipulation tactics are oftentimes quite exploitative and are almost always meant to be insidious and harmful.

Successful manipulation requires three key concepts to happen. These three are:

- Concealing the intentions and behaviors while remaining friendly upfront.
- Understanding the ways, the victim or target is vulnerable and using those vulnerabilities to the advantage of the manipulator.
- Being ruthless enough to not care about the harm caused to the victim.

Manipulation can take several different forms, however, most of them follow the pattern of being covert, harmful, and causing no guilt to the manipulator.

Key Differences Between Manipulation and Persuasion

Ultimately, persuasion and manipulation are quite similar as they are both forms of social influence; however, that is where the similarities end. While persuasion is generally positive, even within dark psychology, manipulation is not. Manipulation is harmful, ruthless, and insidious in every way, shape, and form.

When you are trying to decide whether something is manipulative or persuasive, there are a few questions you can ask yourself to decide. This simple test can allow you to analyze what you are doing and saying to ensure that you are making the choices that work best for you. If you are not looking to manipulate, but the questions tell you that you are erring on the side of manipulation, you know to tone it down a bit, lightening up on the manipulative factors. These questions are:

- What is the intention that has led you to feel the need to convince the other person of something?
- Are you being truthful about your intention and the process?

- How does this benefit the other person?

A persuader attempts to convince the other person from a good place as they intend to help the other person somehow. While a persuader might benefit too, they primarily look out for the other person's best interest. For instance, you may try to convince someone to buy a specific car because it will work better for their family than the car the person is currently looking at. This would be regarded as persuasion because you are offering facts about the other car and showing how it would likely serve the person longer and better.

On the other hand, a manipulator is not concerned with the needs of the other person as they will attempt to push for whatever benefits them the most. Unlike persuasion, the facts offered are likely to be false and intentions completely selfish. For instance, while a persuader may try to convince you with the aim of selling you a car that both fits your needs and gets him his commission, a manipulator on the other hand might use your knowledge of cars, or lack of, to convince you to get a car that will get him a much bigger commission irrespective of if your needs are met or not. The manipulator would rationalize it as something the buyer should know on his own and would not bother pointing out the ways the buyer might be making a bad decision, even if the manipulator knows the decision is wrong.

Chapter 1:
Manipulation and Dark Psychology:
An Overview

MANIPULATION

From a psychological point of view, manipulation is mostly about perception. How we perceive things or actions determines our laws, social formalities, and even our lives.

The manipulator changes these norms with tactics. The determination of the positive or negative connotation of these actions remains subjective, however, psychological manipulation is often considered as devious. Hence, with the subject of dark psychology, we can take into account that the manipulation practiced is often exploitative at the expense of others.

So, what is dark manipulation?

Sources indicate that it is concealment, hiding in the shadows knowing when to strike. It is also a false front that hides true intentions. When we are talking about this level of deception, we are talking about hidden aggression. When we take action, there is a certain level of aggressive behavior that happens. Hence, a small part of manipulation is hiding that aggressive behavior so that the victim sees only good nature.

This is accomplished in various ways and means, one being knowledge. When we allow another to know us, we display vulnerability along with strengths. The knowledge of these personality traits can give the manipulator the ability to maneuver around without any alarms going off.

The effectiveness of manipulating those strengths and vulnerabilities arrives when the practitioner of the dark knows what is vulnerable and what inspires pride.

A reoccurring ideology that drives us to war takes into consideration that war is more negative than positive. We want to avoid it. The manipulation process sees pride in all of us and plays to that pride. For instance, when we use our strength to drive an army to slaughter others, the intention of our pride has been manipulated to enforce the agendas of others.

There is ruthlessness when we talk about psychological manipulation. When dealing with someone other than a pure psychopath who feels little to nothing, ruthlessness can be measured. Often, such ruthless behavior can sneak up on its prey and snag it before it knows what is happening. Harming the prey becomes less than a momentary qualm in the mind of the manipulator.

Often the practitioners of dark psychology use aggression and fear to drive us. Even those whose darkness is not skin deep fall into the category of knowing what weakness is, and how it leaves individuals open to control.

How the manipulator uses that control determines the severity of manipulation. There is and are positive versions of manipulating others like convincing someone that they are not doing well and that they need to get help. However, we are looking at the darker side of manipulation. The manipulator uses their skills of control to get what they want and the cost does not apply.

There are many ways in which an individual or situation can be controlled and changed from positive to negative. psychological manipulators utilize all tactics.

When positive reinforcement is used, the charm is displayed. A forced smile or laughter can trigger laughter in all of us. As when we were infants, we copy what we see. When we see tears, we want them to stop. When we see a smile, we find ourselves smiling as well.

The manipulator using positive reinforcement can shower money, charm, and gifts to get us to feel something. The usage of these things allows us to be controlled on an instinctual level. We follow those who tell us what we want to hear.

Psychological manipulation can also implement negative reinforcement. This is a form of deflection. A substitution of one thing for another.

Often, we have things we need or have to do, but we do not want to do them. The psychological manipulation of negative reinforcement uses the power of negativity to lure the subject from their original need, pushing them toward something they want to be done instead. The long game, a slow play of putting tasks into another's life and then controlling those tasks so that the manipulator can get what they want is an extremely effective and subdued tactic.

Sometimes only partial reinforcement is required to gain control. This is easily achieved by elevating fear and doubts regarding a task. The partial bit is the long play and in the end, the victim will always lose. By slowly planting small seeds of fear and doubt now, victory will eventually happen. An individual trying to work toward something they already were shaky on or had doubts about, will listen to the lie and flow with that idea, and use it to their own destruction.

A partial manipulator only needs to put the thought in the prey's mind; knowing the weakness is already there, and utilizing it will take their prey to a destructive end.

Psychological manipulators favor punishment. From an actual physical lashing to the passive-aggressive playing of the victim, punishment is very effective when one wants to control another.

A manipulator sulks, cries, yells, nags or goes completely silent as a way of blackmailing us; and this instigates guilt in us. As a result, a feeling of "wanting to be the better person" rises to the front, and we find ourselves doing what the manipulator wanted all along.

An individual set on manipulating will use tears, however fake, to bed your will. It is hard to determine the levels of emotion in a person hence making it hard to tell if the tears are real or not. Individuals often fall victim to the crocodile tears of manipulators.

One extreme version of manipulation is violence.

Violence triggers something inside us and we often do anything to avoid it. The manipulator knows that violence strategically applied can make us go into a state of avoidance which incites the control. Physical violence can result to mental scarring caused by the manipulator. Therefore, the manipulator utilizes violence in tactical places to get the result they want. Some would refer to this kind of darkness as 'extreme'.

When it comes to the individual, this can mentally damage them for a long time, if not permanently. However, on a world stage, it can lead to a physical conflict of which might result into genocide.

The manipulation process in dark psychology is normally not a single move; rather it is a series of complex moves, with the outcome only known to the manipulator. Thus, it is safe to say that the motivations of manipulators are as convoluted as human nature.

Usually it is all about the gain. Manipulators of the dark want to gain something. And when we speak about gain, we are talking about power, influence and control over others. The trophy is up to the individual. This can be everything from gaining affections, to money, and even to life itself.

It is about gaining for their personal reasons and gratifications, as well as dominating others and reveling in the power and control they have over them; and this is nothing but extreme selfishness. The mind of the dark practitioner sees the ultimate win as gain over others.

They want power and since superiority is the power over another; taking someone else's power makes them feel superior and this is a huge driving force behind the manipulator. Often, in the case of immature individuals driving manipulations toward superiority, any is pushed aside for just the feeling of being superior.

In relationships, it is about control. The manipulation of power can put one in control. Although we have looked at the role of the vampire and power, and we know who truly has control.

This feeling of control can be overwhelming to the mental state of the dark. Almost drug-like, it is a feeling of emotion that is most logical. Control is one of the easiest manipulation tactics to achieve with only logic to guide. It drives not only the victim but the manipulator as well.

Psychological manipulation can also be about self-esteem. The self-esteem of the manipulator is always in question. Hence, one of the reasons why they manipulate is to define themselves. How easily they are able to manipulate another can tell the dark that they are better than others. That weakness and strength can be measured in the tactical playing field of the hustle.

This defines who they are. Can they manipulate? Yes. Are they stronger? No, they are weaker. It is a measuring device for self-esteem.

However, this is not to say that it is the only device for measurement. Self-esteem can be measured by far less damaging means.

Naturally, the mind gets bored. And what do we do when we get bored? We seek out some form of entertainment. How do we achieve this entertainment? We manipulate—and we all do it.

Let us assume we are bored, and we want to remove or alleviate that boredom with something else. Do we just sit back and wait for something new to happen? No. We actively search for something to replace boredom. Manipulation can take place on many different levels, and have different levels of severity depending on how they are applied;

from picking up a crayon and coloring, taking a mental absence or massacring everyone around you.

The dark psychological manipulator is bored most of the time, more than an average person. The psychological manipulator will often use manipulation to determine their own validity of feelings and emotions. What this boils down to is that manipulation applied in relations with others helps the manipulator regulate reactions to validate or invalidate their own emotions.

The manipulator measures their self-esteem by how others handle their self-questioning. This happens when the practitioner does not have a grasp on what emotions are. They look at their own emotions as invalid and manipulate the situation in such a way that seeks to validate them.

We are stuck with ourselves, and we cannot seem to escape. Psychological manipulators validate or invalidate themselves by the tactical controlling of others. It is an interesting way of viewing life, although there is one form of manipulation that we all idolize.

The con. One of the most common form of manipulation is the art of convincing an individual to transfer their funds to you by tricking them.

This is a hidden agenda of the criminal. This form of mental manipulation preys mostly on the elderly and the rich. However, we all can fall to this form of manipulation. What we choose to spend on and what we do not is our response to a form of psychological manipulation.

Something happens when the buck is passed over. We go from manipulation into action. Something drives us. It is within us, and it is outside forces that drive. What causes this drive and the drive itself is called Persuasion.

DARK PSYCHOLOGY

At its root, dark psychology is all about mind control. You can influence what other people think or do by understanding the inner workings of the other person's mind. You can motivate people to help you by helping them first. You know that they are more likely to offer help if you help them first simply because people tend to reciprocate. When you understand how the minds of those around you work, you can begin utilizing it to your advantage.

USES OF DARK PSYCHOLOGY

Dark psychology is used widely throughout a wide range of scenarios, some of which are more sinister, while others are typically seen as far less harmful. Each of the following groups utilizes concepts included in dark psychology to get desired results: Religion, politics, cults, terrorist organizations, abusers, and salespeople all rely heavily on the concepts of dark psychology, pulling strings behind the backs of other people to get what they want.

- Religion

  Religion is all about conformity. You are required to conform to a certain set of beliefs, into which you are most frequently indoctrinated as children and then encouraged to follow through adulthood. Though it may seem harmless, religion uses several dark psychology techniques to keep people in line and follow the doctrine. Typically, there is some sort of threat of punishment if you do not follow through, it could be going to hell instead of some sort of paradise or heaven after death, or it could be a threat of excommunication and abandonment. These threats play upon two huge fears of people; losing community and a threat of eternal suffering, and as such, people are more likely to obey.

- Politics

  Political leaders often engage in several different dark psychology techniques that are useful in manipulating other people's minds. They carry themselves in certain ways, say certain things that make the people believe they can better empathize, and speak in ways that inspire other people to follow them. They often use slippery slope fear-mongering tactics, promising results that no one will like if people oppose them. They use stances meant to convey power and authority, and people fall for it. People fall for the artificial body language that the politicians use, and the politicians win out.

- Cults

Cults, especially destructive cults, are incredibly exploitative. They are considered totalistic. This means they seek to gain control over the other person entirely. They frequently engage in various forms of thought reform to gain control over the other person's mind. These cults rely on authoritarian following that leads into a wide range of manipulative tactics. Cults rely on their leaders' charisma, deception, isolation, methods of thought-reform, demands for loyalty and devotion, creating a divide between those who follow the cult and outsiders, cult language or jargon that is difficult to understand and follow if you are not a member and as much control as possible over the day-to-day existence of the members. All of this culminates in a group that seeks to manipulate and control the members in a way that demands absolute loyalty. This is how people get sucked in, they are drawn in with false promises, and their personality and thoughts are whittled away, bit by bit, day by day until finally, all that is left behind is a tool for the cult to use. When under the cult's leaders' control, the leader can command nearly anything, and the followers will obey. This makes them so destructive that the members are essentially turned into mindless weapons, willing to do whatever it takes to stay in favor.

- Terrorism

Terrorism groups follow similar methods as cults to get people in line by promising the world for their absolute devotion. They draw people in with idealized values and charismatic leaders and whittle the people away until they are willing to do anything, even if it involves suicide. They see themselves as a part of the whole, a part of the change that they will use to change the world for the better, and they are glad to give their very lives, or the lives of their loved ones, to achieve it.

- Abusers

  Abusers love to utilize dark psychology. They use the inner workings of the minds to weasel their ways into their victims' lives and firmly root themselves as integral members while taking advantage of people's tendencies to want to keep their relationships meaningful. The abuser showers the victim with love, attention, and affection to hook the victim to him before suddenly revoking the attention, making the victim crave it and do anything necessary to get the love back. This sort of manipulation tactic and use of dark psychology is often seen with narcissists, in particular, to understand what the narcissist wants.

- Sales

  Even something as innocent as sales can be littered with dark psychology tactics. The best salespeople can intuitively convince people to buy, tapping into unconscious tendencies, appeals to emotions, and even hijacking the other person's body language to achieve the desired result. Sales people get paid based on their sales, so they will do anything necessary to get the desired results. They will appeal to a parent's fear of a car accident to up-sell to a safer vehicle. They will use a person's near-death experience as a means to segue into selling life insurance. They will change their body language to convince the other person, picking up on small cues here and there and acting upon them to get the desired results.

Understanding Why People Do What They Do: Cracking the Code to Human Behavior:

THE PSYCHOLOGY OF HUMAN BEHAVIOR

For years, researchers have looked into understanding what governs human behavior. How do we reach the decisions that we do? How do we remember or plan for things? These days, wearable technology which is powered by sensors and processes for multi-modal data analysis has enabled researchers around the world to learn about how the human brain works.

The most challenging part of understanding human behavior is figuring out how our brain supports our natural and ever-changing behavior and cognitive processes. This part is more complex as human beings cope with fulfilling evolving physical and mental needs, as well as adapting to our surroundings and environment. The brain is structured in a way that supports all cognitive processes that run simultaneously with the change, and this inevitably translates into our behaviors.

Human behavior is formulated based on a combination of human emotions, actions, and the brain's cognitive function. Action is represented by anything that is either seen or experienced externally through the sight of physiological sensors. When a movie is being filmed and the director says, "Action!" the scene is played out. Actions can occur at any time or range and can vary from the simplest form of reactions like sweating and muscle reactions to food consumption and sleeping patterns.

Emotions are the conscious experiences characterized by mental activities and feelings that develop as a result of rationalizing or prior knowledge. Emotions range from positive to negative, which determines if they are pleasurable or otherwise.

Emotions, as with cognitions, cannot be seen but can be concluded through facial electromyography activity, electrocardiogram, facial expression, galvanic skin responses, or respiration sensors.

Cognitive function, on the other hand, is how you interpret the thoughts that you capture, and they can come in both verbal and nonverbal signals. Thoughts like, "I need to remember to do my grocery shopping later," or "I wonder if my boss is happy with me," are known as verbal cognitions. Nonverbal cognition happens when you picture how your front porch will look like after a renovation.

All three elements; action, emotion, and cognition, are connected in a complex way, but it is through this interrelated system that we learn how to make sense of our world. Through this triad, we learn how to relate to ourselves, which then enables us to decide on the appropriate response or course of action.

THE 3 LAWS OF HUMAN BEHAVIOR

More than 300 years ago, Newton introduced the rest of the world to the three laws of motion. Newton's laws have served as the basis for a countless number of field and lab experiments. These laws have made significant contributions to the innovations and inventions for the industrial revolution and more.

Newton's laws of motion in physics	
LAW #1	A body at rest will remain at rest, and a body in motion will remain in motion unless it is acted upon by an external force.
LAW #2	The force acting on an object is equal to the mass of that object times its acceleration, $F = ma$.
LAW #3	For every action, there is an equal and opposite reaction.

It would certainly be interesting if there was a scientific law that underlined why we behave the way that we do or if there was a formula which could confidently explain why we react in a certain way. But humans, being the complex creatures that we are, have many reasons and methods behind our madness.

However, there are general tendencies which underlie the way that humans behave in general, and these can be classified as the three laws of human behavior.

Law #1: Humans Prefer the Path of Least Resistance

We like our comfort zones. That's why we call them "comfort" zones. We do a lot of our daily routine on autopilot.

Getting out of bed, taking a shower, making breakfast, commuting to work, performing our regular work routine before we clock out for the day and go home.

It would take quite a significant change to jolt us out of the routine we've become comfortable with. This is why change is always difficult, especially in the beginning.

Even when you intend to initiate change for all the right reasons, it's difficult to do. Like when you resolve to start exercising three times a week and go on a diet.

How long does that last before you eventually slip back into your old ways?

It takes sheer willpower and immense discipline to enforce any kind of change, and that's because humans prefer the path of least resistance.

Law #2: We Are Our Behavior

Your behavior is a combination of two things; who you are and your environment. In fact, it was Kurt Lewin who pegged this down as a formula:

$$B = f(P, E)$$

B represents behavior, while P is the person and E the environment. Lewin's formula is presented within his book entitled Principles of Topological Psychology, which was published back in 1936. Lewin proposed this formula to unite the different psychological branches (child, animal, and psychopathology) through a flexible formula which could be applied across all the distinct branches of psychology. This formula relates directly to Lewin's field theory which examines the interaction patterns between an individual and their environment.

Every choice you make from what clothes you plan to wear today to the grocery items you pick, the sights, sounds, smells, people you have around you, all of this has an impact on the way that you behave. Behavior is not an isolated thing, and it takes a combination of both these factors to ultimately dictate how you choose to react at a certain time and place.

What Lewin did was to present us with a formula to work with, but the law is a lot more complex than it seems. Mainly because it's difficult to predict with precision how a person is going to behave or react. When Jane is stressed, for example, she might not order her usual salad at the cafeteria during lunchtime and instead, give in to her impulses and indulge in a less healthy alternative.

However, if the cafeteria was having a lunchtime special on salads, there might be an increase in salad consumption among those within the vicinity having lunch at the same time. Do these two pieces of information bring us one step closer towards knowing what Jane will ultimately choose for lunch? Not at all

The purpose of Lewin's $B = f(P, E)$ formula is to help you acknowledge that you can neither fully predict nor understand what Jane is going to do if you only understand only one side of the equation. You can't predict how Jane is going to act if you only understand how she feels or what she thinks.

At the same time, you can't predict Jane's behavior if you only understand what's happening within her environment. You need to understand both sides of the coin to make the best prediction you can about how Jane is going to behave.

Law #3: Every Choice We Make Has Consequences

Almost everything has pros and cons, and this includes the decisions that you make. Sometimes, you engage in the activity of weighing the pros and cons before you decide. Other times, you jump right in without thinking about the consequences of your actions. Every choice that you make has a cost, benefit or unintended consequence that comes with it; and losses may be experienced in one area while gains are reaped in another.

Here's a scenario to illustrate this point. You're at the pharmacy and you're thinking about purchasing a bottle of vitamins. On the one hand, they could be a placebo, and you start to think about the cons of taking this vitamin. Add that to the fact that you might have to fork out quite a bit of money for it. That gets you thinking about how every dollar you spend on buying this bottle of vitamins (which may or may not work) is a dollar you could have spent on something else.

That gets you thinking, "What do I need to sacrifice/forgo to make this purchase?" This is known as an opportunity cost where you think about the potential tradeoffs to your decision. We tend to fall back on the opportunity cost approach when faced with particularly tough decisions.

Chapter 2:
Common Examples of
Manipulation in Daily Life

Most people assume that they understand the darker aspects of human nature. They imagine they would be able to see manipulators if they met them and know exactly what to do to keep themselves from being taken advantage of. Most people are wrong.

Evil will not wear a mask that makes it easy to identify. In fact, it will do quite the opposite. It will blend in and gain the target's trust before turning on them and victimizing them. The victim will often realize what's going on when it is already too late for them to do anything about it.

The devil himself is known for taking the ideal form or even appearing as an angel of light. Users of dark psychology are no different. They are master shape-shifters that will take whatever form is necessary to snare their prey. Disguise and deception come naturally to them.

So what does one do then?

The best place to start is by educating yourself on their methods. One does not have to use any of them, but they do have to learn enough so they can at least identify the threat when it is present. That is the first step to solving any problem.

The first thing most people don't realize is those dark personality traits are a part of all of us. As such, we all use them to some degree in our daily lives. People around us may even use them on us in ways that are not harmful to us, not realizing what they are doing. Sometimes they may even use them for our own good. For instance, think of mothers telling their kids false facts to get them to eat their vegetables, or trying to trick a drug-addicted loved one to go to a place where they'll find their loved ones waiting to ambush them with an intervention.

Well, this chapter will give you some of the examples that you are most likely to meet throughout your life and highlight many of the tricks they might use on you. It leaves out a lot of the more benign examples of the tricks of dark psychology and tells you of the times when there may be high stakes and you cannot afford to be manipulated or blindsided. These can be moments where someone tries to get you to spend more money than you had intended to, or act in a way that may set you down a path that could be disastrous for you.

THE SECRET TECHNIQUES OF THE BEST ATTORNEYS

They have strong opening cases

A strong opening argument can often be the deciding factor when it comes to winning and losing cases or even closing deals with potential clients. Manipulation is mostly about perception and it becomes a game of controlling perspectives with the way an attorney opens before jurors, judges, and/or potential clients. This can be the crucial moment that determines how the rest of their interactions go.

This is a very important thing to remember when trying to persuade, or prevent being persuaded by an expert attorney. Learning how to take in opening statements, or maybe learning how to give them, can be beneficial when trying to establish a dominant position in a persuasive exchange because that will be the northern star for the rest of the exchange, so remember to open strong and set a firm foundation to build the rest of your persuasion game.

They anticipate the most likely objections

The best attorneys know their own arguments and standpoints so well that they even know the most likely stances people might take against them and prepare to react to those accordingly in advance.

They leave no stone unturned until they are confident that anyone they interact with will leave that exchange feeling like every objection was tended to, and every question answered. Just as it is with manipulators, this is accomplished in various ways and means, one being knowledge. With knowledge of all the parties involved, they easily anticipate arguments from the other party and use that to their advantage.

This can be a fantastic tactic to know how to use when you want to set yourself as an authority in any situation and need to push a certain way of looking at things. Learn to anticipate potential arguments and you will find yourself being harder and harder to refuse when trying to persuade someone.

They use storytelling

Being able to tie stories into logical facts is a brilliant tactic attorneys use because the brain is more likely to enjoy listening to a story and absorb the point being made, more than it will when being inundated with a barrage of facts and statistics.

Stories will often bypass the logical part of the brain and make one think more with their emotions than facts will and this is what you want when trying to establish a strong case for yourself.

As such, you should be careful of someone trying to use this tactic against you and making you fall for a bad argument due to them drawing your logical mind into the nearly hypnotized state that comes with being absorbed by a good story. If you are one easily moved by emotions, then that is an aspect that could be exploited. manipulating those strengths and vulnerabilities is easy when the practitioner knows that you appeal to emotions as opposed to facts. This move increases your suggestibility and reduces your ability to focus on the facts.

They know their audience

Great attorneys make it a point to do background checks on the potential jurors and judges they may have to deal with and try their hardest to make sure they can control who is selected to sit in on their cases. If they can control that element, they try to make their arguments, cases, and general way of communicating suit the audience they will be presenting to.

You never know when you might find yourself in a situation where you have to communicate effectively with people who are not used to your usual style. It is imperative that you know as much as you can about the people you speak to if you are to sway them to come over to your side. You want to learn to communicate with them on their level and avoid the risk of not getting what you want due to minor miscommunications and misunderstandings.

They show and not tell where possible

The mind is more drawn in by stories and pictures than it is by pure facts alone. They are often more interesting and easier for the brain to absorb than dates, studies, and statistics. The best attorneys know this better than anyone and use it to their full advantage. They will present evidence where possible, instead of simply referring to it. They will keep referring back to it, even though the audience knows it's there, to keep reinforcing the 'truthfulness' of their cases and re-establishing themselves as the authority in that specific encounter as they have visual evidence of irrefutable truth. This is about having control, with manipulators, when they have control, then they decide what aspects they want you to know and focus on.

Therefore, you should be aware of someone who is constantly harping on about a piece of evidence they may have shown you. Question it despite seeing it. Make sure that you are not falling for the old trick of misdirection just to be misled by a nefarious manipulator.

They are reasonable

There are moments when digging in your heels and locking your jaw can play against you even when you are in the right. Great attorneys know this and can recalibrate themselves to suit the interaction and better increase the chances of them getting what they want.

You can consider doing this in your own life where you find small points where you agree with your opponent to lower their defenses. Once their guard is down, you can then show them the logic from your point of view.

This can be a great tactic since people are more likely to dig their heels in when it seems force is the only way out, so suddenly changing the game on them can confuse them into thinking they are getting what they want (to be understood by others) while you are secretly just ensnaring them in your trap from a different angle.

They appeal to emotion

There is nothing stronger than being able to use emotions to keep someone off balance and have them eating out of the palm of your hand. Attorneys will often do this by making witnesses angry on the stand to make them slip up in their testimony if it suits them; making a jury feel bad for a defendant whether or not they are guilty; making potential clients trust them, whether it's in the best interest of the client or not.

Make sure to always keep your head and use your opponent's emotions against them where possible. Winning or losing at games of manipulation often comes down to emotions more than they do with facts. Whether you are trying to convince or prevent yourself from being convinced, keeping your emotions in check while making sure your target can not will be the deciding factor in you walking away as the victim or victor in these kinds of insidious games.

They watch the audience's body language

Body language is often a huge deciding factor in how people see you and how they communicate as well. You will often see the best attorneys change their swagger according to the situation so that their message is being communicated on multiple levels. Moreover, body language taps into peoples' mirror neurons and can have their instinct to imitate be used against them.

Mirroring someone's body language can make them feel accepted or slightly intimidated as if you are reacing their minds. Seeing someone mirroring you is often a sign that they are more likely to believe what you are saying. At other times, you want to use this to see how people feel about you and react accordingly where necessary.

Body language skills can be a tool for reading minds and controlling emotions.

They use leading questions

Leading questions is the favorite technique of many people in the legal business because it allows them to control perspectives, which can win or lose cases and future clients.

If someone asks you, "how much dc you hate hockey?" They are not giving you the option of liking hockey. The question already assumes you agree with the person asking it and simply demands the degree to which you agree to show that you are on their side.

Be careful of people using questions like this against you. This tactic can have you not realizing that you are being lured into the trap of accepting a premise that is not true to you. Persuasion is not about right or wrong, it's about winning.

They make sure to stay the course of their arguments

You won't often see expert attorneys getting side-tracked trying to defend non-arguments or even their cignity unless the case depends on it. The best of them will always make it a point to stay the course of their argument while trying to trip up their opposition with the details of their own arguments.

This is a crucial lesson to learn if you want to be more convincing in your own life. You want to be able to make your own statements and arguments seem stable and concrete while subtly destabilizing that of your opponent. You want them abandoning their game to play yours. Once you have them playing your game, you have secured victory. All you need to do is keep them in your world.

THE SECRET TECHNIQUES OF THE BEST SALESPEOPLE

Taking the advisor role

The best salespeople never come across as though they are trying to sell you something right out the gate. They approach as though they are your advisor, guiding you to finding the best product for you.

This is the best way to avoid putting your customer or client on edge and increasing the chances they will buy something. Look carefully at the approach of the next person who tries to sell you something and note how they use this technique to try to put you at ease and make you more suggestible.

Listening skills

The best sales people know how to listen closely for the smallest detail that might help them close the deal. It might be a sign of hesitation, confidence, or anything that tells them if you are a target they should be spending their time on and how they should know if it is time to move on.

Usually, we end up being the ones to give these salespeople all the information they need to handle us better. All they usually have to do is listen as we over-answer simple questions and give ourselves away.

Empathy

A salesperson who can get under the skin of a prospective client is often more likely to have higher sales because they can build a far better rapport with the people they interact with and make them feel safe and secure.

Consider this technique the next time you encounter a salesperson you considered particularly likable. They may just have been using a sense of empathy to comfort you into buying something you may not have wanted in the first place.

Assuming the sale

Salespeople these days no longer ask you if you want to buy their product or not. More often than not they will ask for your details and ask you to sign on the dotted line as if you already agreed to make the purchase.

This often tricks a lot of people into buying things since they don't realize they are being baited into buying something until they're already signing. This tactic is also useful because it takes the choice away from the buyer and puts it in the salesperson's hands.

Confidence

People are a lot more likely to buy with their feelings than with their heads, so a confident salesperson can be highly effective because people are more likely to want to trust them simply because of their confident demeanor.

It's natural to want to follow the lead of someone when they seem like they know exactly where they are going. Salespeople use this information to the fullest by starting the sale with a confident body language that engages you even before any words have been spoken.

Creating a scarcity mindset

The best salespeople know that scarcity and novelty often play a huge role in how we put a value on things. They use this information to make their product seem more valuable by making customers think that this is the best deal they will ever get. They further reinforce this by making customers think that the offer will only stand for a limited time because this is the last one, or another customer showed interest in buying it as well.

Always take your time to know when this pressure is being applied to you or how you could apply it on an unsuspecting victim.

Honesty (where possible)

One of many tactics salespeople have in common with attorneys is their ability to manipulate the truth. They know how to omit certain truths or simply bend the truth where possible to ensure you see the picture the way they want you to.

They will tell the truth where possible and avoid it where necessary. As long as it benefits them, they will play with the truth as much as possible while maintaining a sense of plausible deniability. This way they can practice deception without lying. They can escape on a technicality.

Curiosity

Great salespeople will often use questions that seem simple to get what they want from you. They may disguise these questions as simple curiosity, but they are usually laying the groundwork properly to manipulate you into buying what they want.

In the game of persuasion, information is king. The more you know about a target, the more ammunition you have to bypass their rational mind and appeal to their emotions. No word must be wasted and all information must be treasured.

Adaptability

The best salespeople you ever come across will often behave like chameleons. They will observe you and switch whatever details they need to change about themselves in order to get under your skin and pull you in. They mold their sales pitch around you.

Getting you to feel comfortable enough to listen and give them more and more of your time is a classic sales technique that ensures that nothing as small as beliefs, moods and/or ideologies impede getting what they want; your money.

Communication skills

It is imperative that a salesperson has the gift of the gab and is quick on their feet because the customers will spend more time listening to the way a salesperson speaks more than they do the actual content of their speech.

Therefore, you will often find that the best salespeople will make subtle changes to the way they use language to better appeal to whoever is in front of them at that moment.

Escalating

Escalation is a great tactic that slowly gets you from the sales floor to the office where the papers await your signature. It involves slowly filling your hands with things or carefully orchestrating the tour so that you finally end up at the office, isolated and comfortable.

This also works well after the sale when one might call you and follow up or maybe even try to get new leads through you. Slowly escalating and in turn sets the customer at ease enough to not notice that things are not moving at the pace they intended.

Preparation for objections

As with anything in life, preparation is crucial to being successful. Preparing for possible objections is common among the best attorneys and salespeople. This is a great way to establish and reinforce your position as the expert who needs to be trusted in this given field.

Salespeople take care to make sure they give you the sense that they know more than you and once that has entered your mind, it becomes of the utmost import that they maintain that guise by having all the answers to your questions.

Patience

Patience is a commonly used sales tactic that is seldom recognized by prospective clients. Selling is a process, not an action. The best salespeople will delay you to the point where it becomes a war of attrition.

You could easily be stuck in a salesperson's office for several minutes at a time as they go around finalizing this and verifying that. Do not fall for this trick. It is only to wear down your patience and have you willing to do almost anything to feel the relief of seeing things moving forward, wherever that might lead.

Passion

A passionate and enthusiastic salesman or woman is usually worth a lot to the company they work for because such energetic and positive people can easily sink their hooks into the emotions of their clients and have them follow them down an emotional rabbit-hole that leads them far from the realms of logic where they may easily lose a sale.

Watch out for this kind of approach. Someone coming across as enthusiastic and passionate about what they are speaking about may have that and nothing else. Keep such people focused on the facts and you could find yourself taking the dominant position in these kinds of discussions.

Charm

Charm, much like passion, is a common attribute that a lot of the best salespeople in the game learn to master and weaponize. People are more likely to trust people they feel they get along with than someone they cannot picture themselves enjoying an unrelated social interaction with.

This is one of the oldest tricks in the book as it makes you feel it is permissible to let down your guard and trust the individual in front of you. You do so at your own peril.

THE SECRET TECHNIQUES OF THE BEST LEADERS

Lead with the end in mind

The best leaders always have an agenda that they are trying to accomplish and that often determines their leadership style. They use their goals to determine what it will take to get them to where they want to go and how to keep people following them in that direction.

Since people are drawn to people who seem to have a clear vision of the path ahead, making your vision clear in necessary increments makes people more likely to follow them. Most people feel blind and lost, so the last person they want to follow is someone who is in the dark with them.

Use this knowledge to get others to fall for the allure of your seductive vision and they will follow you to the ends of the earth. Learning to see through the visions of charismatic leaders and asking how their vision helps you is a great way to make sure you never fall for the same spell yourself.

Selective generosity

Great leaders often know how to motivate their followers by creating a healthy sense of competition among those who work under them. One of the best strategies for accomplishing this is using selective generosity. Leaders who know how to complement and reward very carefully often have people feverishly toiling to earn the same spot in the sun.

It is best advised to do this sparsely and almost at random. Never show generosity too easily or the struggle to get it loses its value and you may find people not working with the same level of intensity you may require. Being too predictable about when or to whom you show generosity may make some feel isolated or feel like they may never be on the receiving end of this. To get the most out of this tactic, it is wise to ensure that people believe your gifts are plentiful and can reach the farthest ends of your domain and you will find yourself motivating even the grunts and scrubs who will probably never even get to see you.

Communication and honesty

Honesty is a good quality for any leader to have, but the best leaders understand that perception is everything so they remain selective with the information they share to everyone: friends, enemies or followers. It does not much matter who, but an air of complete honesty can be a great cover concealing your strengths and/or weaknesses.

It is good to remember that there is power in knowing when to appear vulnerable and when to appear strong, but it is always good for those who follow you to think you are always honest with them.

This can be achieved by picking moments where people feel like they can reach you and communicate with you if necessary, but you have to control this so it never works against or inconveniences you. Selectively opening your door to those you lead and knowing when to show weakness to them — but only when it can't be used against you — is a powerful tool in making people feel listened to and feel that they can trust you.

Motivate

Motivation and inspiration are the key qualities that can make or break a leader's run. While the dramatic, impassioned speech is what most people think of when they think of motivating people, it is a series of calculated actions that happen without people even realizing it.

Two great motivating factors are greed and fear. Yes, it is good to be loved where possible, but if being loved is impossible then you can always appeal to these two darker sides of people's personas.

Greed is simple enough. You want to make sure that you make every decision feel like it benefits every party involved and then people will motivate themselves to chase the benefits they believe will come from following you.

Fear is a tightrope act to follow, but it works hand-in-hand with a sense of dependence. If you take time to make sure people you lead know that they need you and why they need you, then the fear of being left alone in the wilderness to fend for their selves will terrify them into action.

Boldness and confidence

One quality that often makes a lot of people feel they can trust someone as a leader is seeing them succeed at taking risks. People often get put into a leadership position purely because they were seen going where no one has gone and lived to tell the tale. You can often see this in a lot of politicians especially. They can often make themselves seem like the shiny beacons guiding the country into a brave new age of conquest or change.

This can be applied in everyday life. If you want people to follow you like so many often do, even when they are duped into voting for a bad presidential candidate, then you should be bold and confident in whatever actions you take and people will be drawn to your courage. They will want to be like you and stick around you in the hopes that they will absorb some of your boldness and ability to get what you want.

Reputation is everything

Perception is everything in the game of manipulation and persuasion. You never want to be seen in a light that makes you seem like anything other than what you want people to believe you are. Too many leaders lose their power just because they did not keep their hands clean and got caught in a scandal.

If you plan on leading, then always make sure that whatever unsavory actions you need to take are never taken in view of the public where your public perception can be tarnished and your reign ruined. Everything from your actions to your clothes must be a message to those around you, an illusion that tells whatever story you want to be told about you.

If you must do something that might put your reputation at risk, then it is best to make sure to give the public something else to look at while you do what you need to do and be swift enough to be finished by the time the distraction has lost its hold of their attention.

Delegation

The best leaders always know how much work they do not need to do themselves. It does not matter if they can do something better. Wasting time trying to do everything will eventually take them away from the goals they strive towards. Delegation saves a lot of time and also has a slightly more sinister potential use. One can always use delegation as a means of getting credit for work they did not do.

Taking all the credit will obviously have negative consequences in the future as more and more people get tired of having credit for their work stolen from them. Taking all the credit is short-sighted. Instead, a good leader shares credit in everything they delegate to those among them.

Taking a little credit for everyone's work saves your time while boosting your worth in the eyes of others.

Discipline

Discipline is a two-edged blade. Great leaders often come across as being the most driven and disciplined people in the company, whether that is true or not. It often serves as a great inspiration to others to keep working hard as well. The other side of that comes when it is time to discipline others.

This can be a great way to keep people in line. Disciplining others should at times be a spectacle that might make others second-guess their own ill-intentions.

This is best used when enemies are crushed completely and their punishment is meted out by a leader who is justified for being hard on those who work against them or do not work to their required standard.

This is a double-edged sword in the sense that it relies on everyone knowing the standard set ahead of time and seeing it be met by the leader. Coldly crushing those who would not meet this standard is a good way to ensure that people fear the very idea of falling out of your good graces.

See adversity as an opportunity

One of the best ways leaders keep themselves and those around them motivated is by making sure they view setbacks as opportunities in disguise. There is nothing that boosts morale than a leader that seems to see the silver lining in every setback and communicates it well.

The very best of leaders never let their followers see them sweat unless it is a calculated move that serves a purpose. They take on the appearance of a solutions-based mindset and surround themselves with people who similarly see things.

Ideas are as contagious as any disease. Make the idea of you being unperturbed by stormy seas and those loyal to you will bravely follow you wherever you choose to lead them. Even if it has to be faked, never let those around you see you stressed or pressured under adversity and you will win their admiration and loyalty.

THE SECRET TECHNIQUES OF THE BEST PUBLIC SPEAKERS

Prepare to make it seem effortless

The last thing you ever see good public speakers doing is trying to be good. They speak as if they are not bothered by where they are or who they are speaking to. It seems completely natural. This is how they win even the toughest of crowds over.

What the audience seldom sees is the hours checking the venue and equipment to make sure nothing plays against them or malfunctions on the day; the hours of rehearsing the speech and gestures so it all seems random and spontaneous on stage; the affirmations and other relaxation and motivation exercises.

They only see the finished product and that truth on the stage is the only one that matters to them; they never see behind the illusion.

Making mistakes

Most of the time you find that few to none of the people in the audience ever know what your speech is supposed to sound like, so there's no point in worrying about making the odd mistake. Great speakers know these two things: 1) the audience is on your side; 2) the mistakes you make on stage are rarely as big, noticeable or memorable as you imagine they'll be.

This is great for helping with nerves, making sure that you don't dwell on the mistakes when you make them, and keep moving forward. Move on as you would in everyday conversation and the audience will soon forget about whatever mistakes you made.

Think about talking, not making a speech

Once great speakers are done with their preparation, they no longer feel the need to actively think about making a good speech. They know that muscle memory will soon kick in and things will come naturally as if they were on autopilot.

A part of this happens in the preparation phases but is vital to remember before hitting the stage as well. The best speakers often make it seem as if their speech is part of an ordinary conversation. The most impressive elements of the speech happen in the preparation/practice phases of the speech. What happens on stage is simply the by-product of this, so there's usually nothing to worry about at this point.

Personalize the message

Some of the best and most captivating speeches are often the ones that tie in a personal story or two. People love stories and nothing better communicates why the content of your speech is important than a story about why it's important to you.

Stories are often easier to remember than facts, so punctuating a fact-dense speech with enjoyable stories regarding or including those facts will not only make them more memorable but will also add a level of sincerity to the speech that most people just can't fake. Don't be afraid to add a touch of authenticity to your speeches by infusing them with a personal story here and there.

Start with the end in mind

Few things are more annoying than speeches that seem to take forever to get to the point. Top public speakers know that by the time they get to the point, the audience will be lost to them. Regaining the audience's attention once it's gone is very tricky to do and often not worth the risk, irrespective of how good the point of the speech was.

It is far better to start with the point and then build the speech around it. Regardless of the topic of your speech, make sure you never risk the point of it being lost to the audience at any point.

Leave them wanting more

There is absolutely nothing wrong with wanting to leave everything on the stage and leaving the audience in awe of you. Unfortunately, this is not a concert you're headlining. If you watch your favorite public speakers closely enough, you will notice that they often leave the speech at a place that feels like a good logical conclusion without having people ever feel like they were getting tired of listening to them speaking.

The best way to never have the audience tire of listening to a speech is to ensure that the same things are repeated in different ways as often as possible. Becoming too repetitive, though necessary, becomes boring and tiring once the pattern of repetitiveness is predictable and/or uninteresting.

Engage the audience

The best speakers on the planet tend to make a talk feel more like a fun conversation than a full-on presentation of ideas. They do this by engaging the audience using things like eye-contact and, sometimes, audience participation.

Looking down at one's notes can be tempting to avoid facing the audience and seeing something that might make you feel self-conscious. Avoid this at all costs. Instead, go around the venue, with your eyes, talking to people individually for a few seconds. This will make them feel they need to give their utmost attention.

Asking the audience questions where possible (it doesn't matter if they're rhetorical at times) can make the audience feel like they are a vital part of the speech and so need to keep listening close in case they have to answer questions as individuals or a group.

Watch body language

Make it a point to watch some of the speeches of your favorite speakers with the volume muted someday. You will probably notice that you can still feel the emotions the speakers are trying to convey without you hearing the words. This is because the best public speakers are very aware of the power of their bodies to sub-communicate their message so they use it to their fullest.

They know they run the risk of giving away some of their private thoughts through their body language so they actively seek to control it instead. This not only enhances their talk but also aids whatever illusion they are trying to keep going while on stage.

Confidence

You probably hear this all the time, but one can never state enough how vital it is to do things with as much confidence as humanly possible. Confidence is not a natural trait for a lot of people, but there are some ways to overcome that.

The majority of one's confidence will often come from feeling secure in the knowledge of one's preparation. Knowing that you did everything you could logically do to prevent things from going awry will give a boost to even the most neurotic person. However, there are still some other methods to consider if this is not enough.

Making use of things like hypnosis, meditation, legal drugs, affirmations etc. can be of great help if you struggle with nerves more than most people.

Simplify the message

If you were invited to give a speech somewhere then there is a good chance that people already respect your authority on that subject. This means that there is no need to go writing a speech that is filled with jargon or other words that are difficult to understand.

Truly great public speakers will do their best to mold their speeches to the audiences so that no one is lost. It is more important to be understood than it is to impress and this is common knowledge among the best public speakers. They are not afraid to let the content they are presenting seem unimpressive while they focus on making sure their talk is engaging and understood by the audience.

Congruency

Giving a speech is every bit as much a viewing experience as it is a listening one. As such, an orator must make it a point that their bodies and voice match every part of their speech.

They look and sound excited when they say something they consider exciting. They sound bored when they say something they consider boring. They will even laugh when saying something they consider funny.

That is congruence — letting the effects of one's words show in the face, body and voice. A lack of congruency can add an element of detachment that might give the impression that there isn't any need to pay attention to your words, ruining what could have been a great speech.

Be passionate

This is probably another point that is stated too often, but that does not make it any less true. Having passion for the subject at hand pouring out of a speaker can have an almost hypnotic effect. The only thing that might match this kind of intensity is the energy that comes from a person giving a speech visibly fighting going off the rails because the topic they're speaking about them fills them with so much emotion and energy. This alone can make a speech so engrossing that forgetting it is no longer an option.

If you ever find yourself in a position where you have to make a speech, make sure it is about something you feel very strongly about or at least approach it in such a way that you end up feeling so strongly about it and your audience will reward you for it.

ADVERTISING AND SUBLIMINAL MESSAGES

The art of persuasion has become a very profitable business in our times, with advertising playing the main role. You are continually being programmed and told what you must eat, what beauty products you should shop for, what insurance you must take up, what medical treatments you must follow, how you need to manage lifestyles and where you need to invest. In fact, the moment you switch on your TV, you are bombarded with commercials trying to convince you which product to buy.

Marketing is built on the principals of manipulation. The tactics used in magazines, billboards, posters, newspapers, free flyers, and television subconsciously tease you because your mind is absorbing all that information. If you see them enough times, you will feel a need for the products. Most marketers unethically manipulate their target audience, creating a sense of attachment to the product. Marketers don't just manipulate adults; they also manipulate children. Most commercials targeted for child-related products are aired on the children's channel or during commercial breaks at a kid's movie. As an adult, you are inclined to indulge your children and find creative ways to celebrate events such as Valentine's Day, which has now become a major commercial event. Marketers prepare for such events weeks ahead.

Beauty pageants, fashion shows, clothing catalogs, and fashion magazines portray perfect-looking models and celebrities who promote models with ideal bodies; thereby targeting teenagers, and giving them the impression that wealth and success are by-products of the slim figure. Hence the many cases of anorexia and bulimia among teenagers and young adults, who are in search of the perfect image at the risk of their health. Marketers exhibit people who are perceived to be beautiful or handsome or celebrities to sell products and earn exorbitant profits. They believe anything can be sold if it appeals to the consumer and is considered attractive. Market manipulation is used to sell the image, manipulating those in search of this perceived image.

The entertaining arts, movies, and music are entertainment enjoyed by most people, but the industry and governments use them as a form of distraction that comes under the category of manipulation. The entertainment industry is controlled by a faction of people who employ specific thought-provoking themes with subliminal messages pulled at your heartstrings, bring tears to your eyes, or terrify you.

Movies about doomsday settings give people an idea of the possibility of something like this happening in the future; here again; you notice consumerism at its best when people flock to buy survival equipment.

Another form of control is to identify those groups which patronize or support a doomsday theory and keep them busy. Many individuals own a survival bag, packed and ready, in the expectation of such an incident. They have platforms like a YouTube channel to talk about this and encourage others to follow suit.

Military invasions, aliens, and zombie apocalypses are some of the examples that you may have witnessed. People have come together to form groups that theorize on these hypothetical events. Artists, no doubt, make a lot of fame and money in this industry by their work and can influence their fans on subjects that they support. So, they are used as tools to impart these types of ideas. These forms of entertainment mask the true nature of the problems the world is facing.

Nicholas West, in his global research post about Predictive Programming, had this to say; he believes predictive programming is real, although many are still in denial. He invites anyone to examine the series of documentaries prepared by Alan Watt and arrive at any other conclusion. Predictive programming originates chiefly in Hollywood, where the large screen can offer a vast vision of where society is heading. You could examine the books and movies which you thought were science fiction or mind-boggling and compare them with society today. "Vigilant Citizen" is a good resource that will make you rethink what "entertainment" is all about.

Music — one of the many powerful art forms — can create mental environments full of good and bad feelings. Some songs would soothe and bring you happiness, whereas some song lyrics can be quite destructive or disturbing to hear, and they target the young and susceptible minds. These songs are more like satanic chants. An example would be the Japanese cult leader who used rhythmic chants to hypnotize his subjects and caused a terrorist event in the subway of Japan, releasing serine gas and injuring hundreds of people.

These groups are disguised to look attractive or "cool." Their themes are mostly seasonal, as they change from time to time to suit the situation and audience, taking advantage of huge concerts and music festivals that keep people distracted from their problems. Music can manipulate our emotions and actively engage an audience.

Extensive psychological research has gone into making music designed to control the workers in a factory or business, so they don't recognize the demands being put on them by their employer for the benefit of the company. The tempo of the tune can speed up to increase productivity, and so on. Elevator music, spa music, and lobby music was also created for a similar purpose; to keep you calm and relaxed.

Soundtracks played at movies can also play on your emotions. Can you recall your own experience of sitting in the dimly lit theatre, anticipating what's to come, and then remember hearing a soundtrack that may have attached itself to a memory playing on your emotions? Good or bad, you may leave the cinema feeling enlightened, influenced, or affected.

MIND CONTROL IN PROPAGANDA AND MEDIA

Political Propaganda is defined as people spreading false information because they support a particular cause. Propaganda is presented negatively, especially when dealing with politicians since they often make false claims so that they can lure citizens into voting for them.

Techniques And How Political Propaganda Works

During the election period, politicians are supposed to campaign. They will talk about what they will do for the citizens. In turn, people will vote for them. After assuming office, the politicians may fail to fulfill their promises. People who are disappointed may vow never to vote for them again. Surprisingly, these same politicians will make use of political propaganda, and people will end up voting for them again.

Present political propaganda techniques have proven to be greatly effective. Nowadays, people making use of political propaganda are focusing on symbolism. When targeting the mind of a voter, you should also hit their heart. Politicians will also make use of generalizations, and they will make sure that some things sound great. On the surface, things may look good, but when you dig deeper, you will realize that the people making use of propaganda are trying to deceive all their followers.

The Tools Of Propaganda

A propagandist will always make use of certain tools so that they can mobilize some followers. The most important tool is suggestion, and it aligns with stimulation. The propagandists will stimulate other people to accept all they have to say without challenging their assertions. Since stimulation is a propaganda device, it makes sure that people can accept all the propositions that are brought forth without even thinking logically.

The propagandist will make use of this tool by coming up with some positive statements that are meant to entice a group of people. They will always present their statements using a familiar language, and they will ensure that they have incorporated simplicity in each instance. By failing to admit the reality, the propagandist will be able to amass a huge following.

Suggestion is also known to be used in the advertising sector. Another commonly used tool is insinuations, hints, and indirect statements. The best example, in this case, is the advertising sector. One example is political advertisements, which are often pure propaganda with manipulated "facts" or outright deceptions.

Another tool is when a propagandist focuses on learning more about people, in order to know how to appeal to and manipulate their target audience.

Looking Into Social Media Tools

Social media ensures that people can keep in contact through the use of applications such as Facebook. For instance, there is a group of young individuals that learned about the Tinder dating app, and they began to influence their colleagues. With time, some of the conversations within the platform would be more about politics.

On various social media sites, certain propagandists send messages targeting various voters with misinformation. The users of these sites had agreed to the terms and conditions while signing up. It is not clear how many candidates manage to win elections by carrying out social media campaigns.

Nowadays, social media is among the online applications that are widely used. About 70 percent of adults in the United States have signed up on Facebook. A high percentage of the people who signed up on Facebook and other social media applications log into these platforms regularly. A majority of these people are also not using social media platforms for politics; rather, they use these platforms for self-expression, reading articles, and sharing content.

Social media has become common, and it is now a major part of people's lives. It is also trusted, unregulated, and targetable. Since social media has attracted a considerable population, politicians were bound to make use of such tools during the election period. There is a substantial amount of evidence that social media is being used to deceive and manipulate voters.

Since technology has also advanced greatly, the news feed is also automated, and that means that the politicians may focus on manipulating different social networks. The best example, in this case, is how about half of the Twitter conversations globally usually originate from bots. Some of these accounts contain a substantial amount of political content. The political content has been well crafted, such that the targets will not realize that they are interacting with a bot.

Some of these bots have been used in other nations such as Brazil during the election period. The bots were used during the period when one of the presidents was being impeached. They came in handy when carrying out the impeachment campaign. Also, the bots were used during the mayoral race that took place in Rio. The majority of political leaders are also making use of social media tools, especially in young democracies that are utilizing automation in a bid to spread information.

Psychological Warfare: Don't Be Manipulated

When it comes to manipulation, the manipulator will always focus on getting what they want, using various forms of trickery. Many people believe that manipulation is immoral. Since psychological manipulators use various deception techniques, we will look into each of these tactics and offer a suitable solution on how people can defend themselves in case of any eventuality.

Method 1 – Gaining Manipulation Skills

- **Take An Acting Class**

  When it comes to manipulation, it is good to learn more about how to master emotions while making sure that other people can become receptive, whenever you tend to become emotional. To learn more about expressing yourself using various techniques that play on people's emotions, it is good to enroll in an acting class. While in an acting class, it will be possible to gain some powers of persuasion. Always focus on the main goal, which involves understanding the methods of manipulating people, so you can protect yourself.

- **Enroll in a Public Speaking Class**

  Acting classes are meant to make sure that you can master your emotions and learn how you display them. Enrolling for a debate class is advisable so that you can learn more about convincing other people about your argument. You will learn more about how to clearly organize your thoughts. Additionally, a public speaking class will also enlighten you about how to sound convincing. A manipulative person will use these skills to influence the actions of others by convincing them to do what they want.

- **Come up with Similarities**

  Manipulators always make sure that they have learned more about the body language of their target victims. They also look into the intonation patterns of their victims before they can proceed with the manipulation process. Eventually, the manipulators will come up with persuasive methods, and they will also appear calm. Watch out for this type of behavior.

- **Being Charismatic**

  Charismatic individuals often have a way of getting what they want. When understanding how charming people can manipulate others, you will have to ensure that you have worked on your own charisma. Not everyone who is charismatic is manipulative, so you need to pay attention to understand who is sincere and who is misleading you. You should also be able to smile, and your body language should showcase that you are approachable, so that people feel they can easily approach you and talk to you. You must also be able to initiate a conversation with any individual, regardless of various factors, such as age.

  Some of the techniques that you can utilize to become charismatic include ensuring that people feel special. The best way to achieve this is by maintaining eye contact while conversing with a person. Make sure that you have also initiated a discussion about how they feel and the interests that they have. Always show the other person that you care, and you want to learn more about them. An insincere charismatic person will pretend to care about the other person, even when they don't.

  Maintaining high levels of confidence is necessary as charismatic people are always passionate about everything that they do. Hence, it is advisable to have confidence in yourself.

- **Learn from the Masters**

  If you have a friend who happens to be a psychological manipulator, you should observe them and also take notes, so you know what to look out for from potential manipulators. Always carry out a case study and ensure that the manipulators are the main point of focus. It will be possible to learn a lot from them. Pay attention to how these individuals get what they want. They may also share some insight into how they manipulate people. The main issue is that you might end up being tricked, but you will gain some insight into how to manipulate people effectively, and therefore how to avoid being manipulated.

- **Learn More about How to Read People**

Each individual has a psychological and emotional makeup, and it always varies from one individual to another. When you learn about the psychological and emotional makeup of a person, it will be possible to manipulate them. Manipulative people will often learn more about the individual that they are going to manipulate, and in many cases, they become trusted by the person before they slowly take advantage of them.

Some of the things that you may notice as you try to understand people include the realization that most people are vulnerable, and it is possible to reach out to them by evoking their emotional responses. For instance, some people may cry when watching a movie, and they may showcase high levels of sympathy and empathy. For a person to manipulate such individuals, they often joke around with their emotions while also pretending to feel sorry, and they will eventually get what they want by playing on the other person's emotions.

Other people have a strong sense of guilt. Most of the individuals who have a guilt reflex grew up in a restrictive household, and they may have been punished for every wrong deed that they committed. Manipulators may make sure that the person feels guilty about various acts, so they are more likely to give in to a manipulator's demands at the end of it all.

Some people usually respond to rational approaches. For example, if you have a close friend who is always logical and always keeps up with the news that means that they are always after verifiable information. In such an instance, a manipulative person will make sure that they have utilized their persuasive powers accordingly when manipulating them.

Method 2 – Using Different Manipulation Techniques

- **Impose an Unreasonable Request, Then Present a Reasonable One**

This is a technique that has proven to be very effective, and many manipulators often use it. It is also shockingly simple. Whenever a person wants to manipulate someone, they come up with a request that is not reasonable. The other person will reject the unreasonable request, and in that instance, a reasonable request is presented. The new request should be appealing to the individual who is being targeted. The best example to use in such a case is when an employee may not accept a permanent request to arrive early at work, but they will voluntarily accept a request whereby they are supposed to arrive at work early over a specific period to handle various urgent duties. The employee will prefer engaging in a short-term request since it is less cumbersome when compared to the long-term request.

PERSONAL RELATIONSHIPS

Manipulation is also present in relationships. Some people manipulate their friends for their selfish gain. Boyfriends use mind control on their partners to achieve their set target. Husbands also use manipulation on their wives in order to control them.

However, it should be noted that long-term manipulation can cause adverse effects on close relationships between friends, family members, or romantic partners. It can deteriorate the real essence of the relationship and can even lead to the dissolution of such a relationship.

In intimate relationships, manipulation can come in the form of secret-affairs, flattery, over-displaying affection and many more.

People may also feel manipulated in a relationship that has become toxic. In a casual friendship, one person may be using the other to meet their own selfish goals. The manipulator may be the louder one, controlling the other to do their bidding but when it comes to what concerns the other; they find a way to extricate themselves. The tactics they use involve coercion, favors, use of guilt, lending money amongst other things.

- **Coercion**: Friends use coercion to manipulate one another into doing what they need them to do. They may beat them up, threaten them or to a higher degree, involve and threaten their loved ones. For instance, a group of friends were involved in a theft. When they were apprehended and questioned, one opened up that he never wanted to go with them. In fact, that was his first time. He agreed to go with them because they had been bullying him daily. When he wouldn't give in to them, they resorted to harassing his sister and he couldn't take it. So, he had no choice but to give in to their demands.

- **Favors:** Doing favors is another deadly technique used in friendship manipulation. A friend of mine had a habit of asking "hope all these are not to deceive me so as to do another for me" whenever someone did him a favor. Friends, especially the manipulative ones know how to get their target. They know what they want and as such, they do it for them without being asked, claiming "what are friends for?" However, they would later demand for a favor in return and their favors are usually huge with underlying selfish interests. At this point, it then becomes difficult to say no.

- **Money Lending:** Money lending can be another means of becoming the manipulator amongst your friends. Check your group of friends; you would agree with me that the one that spends more is usually the one at the helm of affairs. He dictates "who does what?" most times. This is because he is the purse of the group. He lends money individually to the members of the group; hence, he can exert some sort of control over them.

MANIPULATION AT WORKPLACE

Many people deal with workplace manipulation at some point in their career. Sometimes it is because one of their co-workers is a manipulator while other times it is everyday forms of manipulation. For example, a co-worker manipulates you into helping them with their task or gets you to do their task. They only do this because they don't like this specific responsibility.

Sometimes you will start to notice your supervisor is a manipulator. Unfortunately, this is highly common in the workplace as many supervisors have used manipulation to get their position, especially if they worked themselves up the ladder. However, you should never assume your supervisor is manipulative. If they are, they will typically demonstrate signs of being a manipulator, such as bullying, blaming others, guilting their staff, giving staff the silent treatment, and distorting facts.

One way you know if you work with a manipulator is by the way you are treated. Manipulators need to make sure you know your place, meaning you are beneath them. Therefore, they will often make sarcastic comments that make you feel inferior. For example, you come to work one day in professional attire that is more casual than what your company usually wears. Instead of a white shirt and a suit, you are wearing a white shirt with slacks. When your co-worker notices your attire, they start to belittle your clothes, making fun of your lower-paying income and that you can't afford nicer clothes.

How To Use Manipulation In Workplace And Business?

Words such as psycho-tricks, manipulation or psycho-games cause indignation. No one is happily manipulated. The problem is that psycho-tricks are part of everyday life and whether you like it or not, they are used daily, in private and professional life and by many people.

This usually happens involuntarily and results from childhood behavior patterns. You also use psycho-tricks regularly, be it consciously or unconsciously — that's guaranteed — so why not use the harmless psycho games to achieve your goals or become more popular?

Basically, whenever there is an ulterior motive behind your actions, a form of manipulation takes place. You would never subjugate your fellow human beings to your psycho-games unless you acted selflessly every single second of every day. Think this is true for you? Presumably, there will hardly be a man who can affirm this question in the best conscience.

Manipulation describes a "form of influencing others for their benefit", as used for example in advertising psychology.

In the end, we want the partner to act in our favor and go to the movies with us on Friday night, even if the cozy round of friends would be more fun for him.

We want our counterparts to be happy about a gift, to say thank you and perhaps to like us a little bit more than they already do. Or would you not be angry, if a simple "thank you" was not said to you or maybe the gift or your person was criticized?

Finally, we also wish for appreciation, recognition and maybe even career advancement in the workplace.

People are social beings and as a result, masters of psycho-games.

Almost everyone manipulates their social environment simply because of our history. People are social and this used to be vital for our "species" and has not changed even today. High-quality social relationships are the most important factor of happiness in a person's life. Accordingly, loneliness is a guarantee of misfortune, which can even lead to death.

So it is in our instincts that we want to get along well with other people. At the same time, in every social grouping, the individual always threatens to perish. Who does not learn to stand against the "stronger", is quickly exploited or ignored.

This applies both in the job and in all other areas of life. Therefore, we develop mechanisms in childhood to enforce our will against the "stronger" who might be the parents or siblings.

And fortunately, we are cultured enough nowadays not to always carry out such "power games" through physical arguments, instead, each person develops his manipulation strategies, such as emotional blackmail, pity, defiance, flattery, and an appeal to the conscience among other strategies.

Reflect Your Individual Psycho-Tricks

Keep your eyes peeled in the near future and be mindful of psycho-games - both in yourself and in your social environment.

Learn to distinguish between negative and harmless manipulation and discard harmful behaviors. Still, it can be exciting to experiment a bit with psycho-games.

There is indeed a positive form of manipulation. For example, you can learn more about the behaviors and characteristics of the other person, or make them like it. Sounds exciting? It is.

That's why we have put together various psycho-tricks for you that you can test out with a clear conscience in the professional world — and perhaps sharpen your awareness of the topic of psychological manipulation.

These psycho games may help you achieve your career goals. First and foremost, however, they ensure that your colleagues and supervisors like you more, and this creates a better working atmosphere and pulls you together. But please do not overdo it, because manipulation is and remains a fine line!

Psycho Game 1 Imitation

Imitate your counterpart. This means inconspicuously detecting small gestures of your interlocutor, taking his posture or repeating what he said. The emphasis is on "unobtrusive".

Your counterpart should not consciously perceive the imitation. Instead, his mirror neurons respond to your imitation, creating a sense of sympathy whose origin he cannot explain to himself. This mechanism is called a resonance phenomenon and results from the so-called mirror neurons.

Even if this kind of imitation sounds strange to you, it is a part of everyday life. The mirror neurons unconsciously ensure that we imitate people - especially those whom we find sympathetic. As a result, your counterpart feels understood and taken seriously and also feels a higher degree of sympathy. Just try it and in the next meeting, pay close attention to which people in the room might be imitating your posture.

Psycho-Game 2 "Foot in The Door"

The so-called "foot-in-the-door technique" is also a mechanism that you have certainly unconsciously used. It is quite simple. Ask a person for a favor. Start with tiny little things that your opponent can not refuse at all.

The crux of the matter is that while the person does you a favor, it makes you feel appreciated. The fact that you seek their help or their advice testifies to their confidence and thereby increases their self-esteem.

Strange as it may sound, this creates a kind of win-win situation. His positive self-image as a "helper" then ensures that this person is more likely to fulfill you, larger pleasures more likely. But please do not overdo it. If necessary, offer your help as well. This is how true teamwork works.

Psycho Game 3 Advance

Another psycho-game, which has to do with favor, is the advance performance. So if you "give" something to a person, be it a favor, a present, or just your time and helpfulness, they will automatically go on the defensive.

Most people do not like such an "imbalance" and therefore insist on giving you such a favor, giving a gift, or repaying in any other way. So, if you want something from a human being in the future, first go into this preliminary performance. Life is known to consist of giving and taking.

Psycho Game 4 Compliments

Have you ever complimented a person? Then you actually manipulated him. If you notice, for example, that the colleague has lost weight, and you express that with a compliment, it proves to be interesting and interesting to your counterpart. He realizes that you are well-disposed to him and will immediately classify you as sympathetic.

However, this only works for serious compliments. Now, if you shower compliments on any person crossing your path, you are more "slimy", fake, and have selfish ulterior motives with your kind words. Here, too, it depends on the right degree.

Psycho Game 5 Secrets

If you want to get closer to a person on a friendly level in no time, just tell him a secret. This creates a feeling of togetherness. The fact that you share this secret with this person is a sign of trust and thus creates sympathy with your counterpart.

You have the feeling of a "special connection". In professional life, you should, of course, make sure that it is an innocuous mystery. After all, you always have to expect that it will come to light sooner or later - and then it should not be embarrassing or even dangerous for your career.

Psycho Game 6 Mass Pressure

The more people pursue one goal, the more attractive it will be to others. That is simply the fact and result of our evolution. Humans are herd animals and are therefore reluctant to swim against the current.

Suppose you want to become a manager. So now you just have to convince your teammates and supervisors that this decision will bring benefits to everyone involved. The more people support your project, the more attractive it will look to outsiders - maybe even the final decision-makers.

So, learn to gain "allies" for your projects, and you'll be more likely to achieve all of your goals in the future as well as faster. This applies to great success as well as to small projects.

Psycho Game 7 Powerful "No"

You are always in a good mood and always have a joke in the store? Then you are certainly popular, but your career could stall. Although people are attracted to positive personalities, which relax their daily work and put a smile on their faces, they tend not to take them seriously.

A candidate for promotion is not necessarily the office clown. So if you want to be successful in business, sometimes you also show your serious and authoritarian side. A clear "no" can already cause small miracles and you will notice directly how you are given more respect.

Psycho Game & Rarity

What is in abundance becomes uninteresting. However, people appreciate something that is rare more. That too is in their nature. This works with material things as well as with immaterial or even persons.

So, if you want to be valued more, you sometimes go off the field. Spend the lunch break with a colleague in the café instead of always with everyone else in the canteen.

Participate only in important meetings and are not always available. This makes you more directly interesting and "important". But do not overdo it, otherwise, you will become an outsider and achieve exactly the opposite of your actual intention. Here is a little tact needed.

DIFFERENT TYPES OF MANIPULATOR

People dissatisfied with their social, loving, professional and family lives are real oceans of possibility for manipulators to exercise their "talents". There are different forms of manipulation, one for each situation:

The Idiot: This word is not very well known. Deceiver, liar, and crook are the meanings. The talkative manipulator has political, financial, and even sentimental goals.

The Brute: The rough manipulator has psychological problems, owners of narcissistic and perverse personalities. It makes their victims feel emotionally dependent.

The Good: Unlike the other modalities, the good manipulator believes that he has noble feelings and that he can change the world according to his rectitude of character.

BEHAVIORAL TRAITS OF FAVORITE VICTIMS OF MANIPULATORS

There are certain characteristics and behavioral traits that make people more vulnerable to manipulation and people with dark psychology traits know this full well. They tend to seek out victims who have those specific behavioral traits because they are essentially easy targets. Let's discuss 6 of the traits of the favorite victims of manipulators.

Emotional insecurity and fragility

Manipulators like to target victims who are emotionally insecure or emotionally fragile. Unfortunately for these victims, such traits are very easy to identify even in total strangers, so it's easy for experienced manipulators to find them.

Emotionally insecure people tend to be very defensive when they are attacked or when they are under pressure and that makes them easy to spot in social situations. Even after just a few interactions, a manipulator can gauge with a certain degree of accuracy, how insecure a person is. They'll try to provoke their potential targets subtly, and then wait to see how the targets react. If they are overly defensive, manipulators will take it as a sign of insecurity, and they will intensify their manipulative attacks.

Manipulators can also tell if a target is emotionally insecure if he/she redirects accusations or negative comments. They will find a way to put you on the spot, and if you try to throw it back at them, or to make excuses instead of confronting the situation head-on, the manipulator could conclude that you are insecure and therefore an easy target.

People who have social anxiety also tend to have emotional insecurity, and manipulators are aware of this fact. In social gatherings, they can easily spot individuals who have social anxiety, then target them for manipulation. "Pickup artists" can identify the girls who seem uneasy in social situations by the way they conduct themselves. Social anxiety is difficult to conceal, especially to manipulators who are experienced at preying on emotional vulnerability.

Emotional fragility is different from emotional insecurity. Emotionally insecure people tend to show it all the time, while emotionally fragile people appear to be normal, but they break down at the slightest provocation. Manipulators like targeting emotionally fragile people because it's very easy to elicit a reaction from them. Once a manipulator finds out that you are emotionally fragile, he is going to jump at the change to manipulate you because he knows it would be fairly easy.

Emotional fragility can be temporary, so people with these traits are often targeted by opportunistic manipulators. A person may be emotionally stable most of the time, but he/she may experience emotional fragility when they are going through a breakup, when they are grieving, or when they are dealing with a situation that is emotionally draining. The more diabolical manipulators can earn your trust, bid their time, and wait for you to be emotionally fragile. Alternatively, they can use underhanded methods to induce emotional fragility in a person they are targeting.

Sensitive people

Highly sensitive people are those individuals who process information at a deeper level and are more aware of the subtleties in social dynamics. They have lots of positive attributes because they tend to be very considerate of others, and they watch their step to avoid causing people any harm, whether directly or indirectly. Such people tend to dislike any form of violence or cruelty, and they are easily upset by news reports about disastrous occurrences, or even depictions of gory scenes in movies.

Sensitive people also tend to get emotionally exhausted from taking in other people's feelings. When they walk into a room, they have the immediate ability to detect other people's moods, because they are naturally skilled at identifying and interpreting other people's body language cues, facial expressions, and tonal variations.

Manipulators like to target sensitive people because they are easy to manipulate. If you are sensitive to certain things, manipulators can use them against you. They will feign certain emotions to draw sensitive people in so that they can exploit them.

Sensitive people also tend to scare easily. They have a heightened "startle reflex," which means that they are more likely to show clear signs of fear or nervousness in potentially threatening situations. For example, sensitive people are more likely to jump up when someone sneaks up on them, even before they determine whether they are in any real danger. If you are a sensitive person, this trait can be very difficult to hide, and malicious people will be able to see it from a mile away.

Sensitive people also tend to be withdrawn. They are mostly introverts, and they like to keep to themselves because social stimulation can be emotionally draining for them. Manipulators who are looking to control others are more likely to target people who are introverted because that trait makes it easy to isolate potential victims.

Manipulators can also identify sensitive people by listening to how they talk. Sensitive people tend to be very proper; they never use vulgar language, and they tend to be very politically correct because they are trying to avoid offending anyone. They also tend to be polite, and they say please and thank you more often than others. Manipulators go after such people because they know that they are too polite to dismiss them right away; sensitive people will indulge anyone because they don't want to be rude, and that gives malicious people a way in.

Empathic people

Empathic people are generally similar to highly sensitive people, except that they are more attuned to the feelings of others and the energy of the world around them. They tend to internalize other people's suffering to the point that it becomes their own. In fact, for some of them, it can be difficult to distinguish someone's discomfort from their own. Empathic people make the best partners because they feel everything you feel. However, this makes them particularly easy to manipulate, which is why malicious people like to target them.

Malicious people can feign certain emotions, and convey those emotions to empathic people, who will feel them as though they were real. That opens them up for exploitation. Empathic people are the favorite targets of psychopathic con men because they feel so deeply for others. A con man can make up stories about financial difficulties and swindle lots of money from empathic people.

The problem with being empathic is that because you have such strong emotions, you easily dismiss your doubts about people because you would much rather offer help to a person who turns out to be a lair than deny help to a person who turns out to be telling the truth.

Emphatic people have a big-hearts, and they tend to be extremely generous, often to their detriment. They are highly charitable, and they feel guilty when others around them suffer, even if it's not their fault and they can't do anything about it. Malicious people have a very easy time taking such people on guilt trips. They are the kind of people who would willingly fork over their life savings to help their friends get out of debt, even if it means they would be ruined financially.

Malicious people like to get into relationships with emphatic people because they are easy to take advantage of. Emphatic people try to avoid getting into intimate relationships in the first place because they know that it's easy for them to get engulfed in such relationships and to lose their identities in the process. However, manipulators will doggedly pursue them because they know that once they get it, they can guilt the empathic person into doing anything they want.

Fear of loneliness

Many people are afraid of being alone, but this fear is more heightened in a small percentage of the population. This kind of fear can be truly paralyzing for those who experience it, and it can open them up to exploitation by malicious people. For example, many people stay in dysfunctional relationships because they are afraid, they will never find someone else to love them if they break up with an abusive partner. Manipulators can identify this fear in a victim, and they'll often do everything they can to fuel it further to make sure that the person is crippled by it. People who are afraid of being alone can tolerate or even rationalize any kind of abuse.

The fear of being alone can be easy to spot in a potential victim. People with this kind of fear tend to exude some level of desperation at the beginning of relationships, and they can sometimes come across as clingy. While ordinary people may think of being clingy as a red flag, manipulative people will see it as an opportunity to exploit somebody. If you are attached to them, they'll use manipulative techniques to make you even more dependent on them. They can withhold love and affection (e.g., by using the silent treatment) to make the victim fear that he/she is about to get dumped so that they act out of desperation and cede more control to the manipulator.

The fear of being alone is, for the most part, a social construct, and it disproportionately affects women more than men. For generations, our society has taught women that their goal in life is to get married and have children, so, even the more progressive women who reject this social construct are still plagued by social pressures to adhere to those old standards. That being said, the fact is that men also tend to be afraid of being alone.

People with abandonment issues stemming from childhood tend to experience the fear of loneliness to a higher degree. There are also those people who may not necessarily fear loneliness in general, but they are afraid of being separated from the important people in their lives. For example, lots of people end up staying in abusive or dysfunctional relationships because they are afraid of being separated from their children.

Fear of disappointing others

We all feel a certain sense of obligation towards the people in our lives, but some people are extremely afraid of disappointing others. This kind of fear is similar to the fear of embarrassment and the fear of rejection because it means that the person puts a lot of stock into how others perceive him or her. The fear of disappointing others can occur naturally, and it can be useful in some situations; parents who are afraid of disappointing their families will work harder to provide for them, and children who are afraid of disappointing their parents will study harder at school. In this case, the fear is constructive. However, it becomes unhealthy when it's directed at the wrong people, or when it forces you to compromise your comfort and happiness.

When manipulators find out that you have a fear of disappointing others, they'll try to put you in a position where you feel like you owe them something. They'll do certain favors for you, and then they'll manipulate you into believing that you have a sense of obligation towards them. They will then guilt you into complying with any request whenever they want something from you.

Personality Dependent disorders and emotional dependency

Dependent personality disorder refers to a real disorder that is characterized by a person having an excessive and even pervasive need to be taken care of. This need often leads the person to be submissive towards the people in their lives and to be clingy and afraid of separation. People with this disorder act in ways that are meant to elicit caregiving. They tend to practice what's called "learned helplessness." This is where they act out of a conviction that they are unable to do certain things for themselves, and they need the help of others.

Such people have a hard time making decisions, even when dealing with simple things like picking out which clothes to wear. They need constant reassurance and advice, and they let others take the lead in their own lives. These are the kinds of people who either move back into their parents' homes as adults or treat their spouses and partners as though they are their parents.

Manipulators like to target people with dependent personality disorders because they are very easy to control and dominate. These people willingly cede control over their lives to others, so when manipulators come knocking, they don't face much resistance. Manipulators start by giving them a false sense of security, but once they have won their trust, they switch gears and start imposing their will on them.

Emotional dependency is somewhat similar to dependent personality disorder, but it doesn't rise to the level of clinical significance. It stems from having low self-esteem, and it's often a result of childhood abandonment issues. People with an emotional dependency will play the submissive role in relationships for fear of losing their partners. They tend to be very agreeable because they want to please the people in their lives. Such people are easy to manipulate, and malicious people can easily dominate them.

Chapter 3:
Most Common Manipulation Techniques

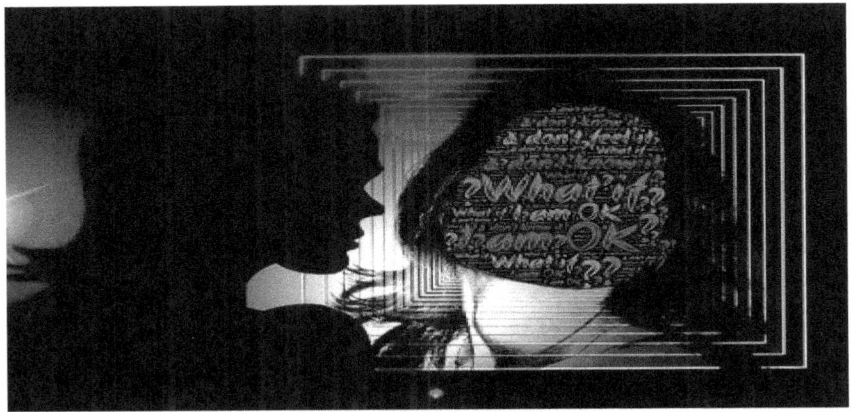

Dark psychology employs a vast range of tactics designed to make targets doubt themselves to the point of being willing to follow the manipulator's lead. Some of these tactics are more insidious and covert, such as passive-aggression, whereas others, such as threatening an individual to get the desired result is far more noticeable. Ultimately, manipulators typically need a wide range of tools to effectively manipulate someone. By having a variety of tactics, a manipulator is nearly guaranteed to have a strategy for any given situation.

Love-Bomb and Devaluation Cycle

The love-bomb and devaluation cycle can essentially destroy a person's sense of self-worth. This is typically used in relationships to keep people under control and involves two steps: Love-bombing, then devaluing. Oftentimes, the cycle will continue to repeat, over and over, in an effort to keep an individual just invested enough in the relationship to put up with the abuse.

Love-Bombing

The love-bomb stage involves idolizing the person the predator seeks to manipulate. Through sweet words, flattery, gifts, and other tactics meant to increase feelings of intimacy and bonding. The predator may seek to spend more time with the target, insisting on lavish dates, kind words, and being the perfect gentleperson. Any information learned about the target, particularly that information about the individual's likes and desires in a person, are put into play here. The manipulator will act according to the target's desires and, in a sense, provide what the target wants, albeit temporarily.

The frequency and intensity of love-bombing typically increase quite quickly, far quicker than is normal within most healthy, boundary-respecting relationships and this is intentional. It creates a sense of a whirlwind romance that the target quickly latches onto as if becoming addicted to the intensity and the good feelings that are quickly associated with the manipulator.

Devaluation

When the predator is sufficiently satisfied that the target is invested enough in the relationship, the devaluation stage begins. The manipulator will suddenly and unexpectedly change tactics, instead of discarding and devaluing the target. The purpose of this is similar to loosening the line of a fishing pole when reeling a fish in. The person suddenly feels inclined to chase after the manipulator so as to stay in his or her good graces. Suddenly lacking the adoration that the target has grown accustomed to, he or she will desperately try to earn that back when met with devaluation, playing right into the manipulator's trap.

Gas lighting

Yet another major manipulation tactic is gas lighting. In gas lighting, the manipulator will entirely deny something that has happened so innocently, convincingly, and normally that the person being gas lighted will believe it. This has the result of convincing the target that his or her perception of reality may not be accurate or should not be trusted, which typically results in the target deferring to the manipulator's judgment. Consider an interaction in which Alex and Brenna are talking with each other. Alex says something that implies that Brenna needs to learn to listen and defer to him because of gender roles. He may say something like, "Do your job," implying she should obey him. If she were to call him out on this behavior and accuse him of being sexist, he would tell her that she is misunderstanding him and that he never said that. With plenty of different instances of being told she does not understand what has happened, she eventually comes to believe what Alex is saying and deferring to his judgment. She is left feeling doubtful about her ability to rationally perceive the world around her and then decides to trust what Alex says as fact.

Gas lighting sometimes happens with phrases such as, "that never happened," "it is all in your imagination," and "are you okay? You seem out of it." All of these are designed to instill doubt in the target. The person being gas lighted is stuck between two different contradictory beliefs, wondering if the other person is trustworthy, or if their sense of self and reality is trustworthy. In manipulation, the predator will always seek to be seen as trustworthy, forcing the other person into believing they are losing their mind.

Projection

Projection is a commonly used defense mechanism in which the manipulator projects whatever another person is accusing them off onto the other person instead. Think of someone who is being confronted with accusations of being abusive. The manipulator would then turn it around to point at the accuser's behaviors, picking at anything that could remotely be construed as abusive and latching onto it. He or she may cherry-pick at events, potentially taking them out of context so they can be tweaked to his or her own benefit. Imagine the manipulator saying that the accuser is abusive because, at one point, the accuser yelled at the manipulator. The manipulator brings this up but conveniently avoids bringing up that he had been instigating, poking at the accuser to provoke such a reaction in the first place. In this case, by shifting the narrative, the manipulator has put the accuser on the defensive instead of offensive.

While frequently done in order to derail arguments and accusations, it is sometimes done unconsciously as well, with the manipulator projecting faults onto other people to avoid responsibility for them. If the manipulator is accusing the other person of being abusive, he may be trying to avoid blame for his abusive behaviors. If he can point at someone else being abusive, he is able to shift things so they are no longer one-sided.

Distractions

Sometimes, manipulators seek to distract their targets with all sorts of trains of thought or attacks. This disarms the target, particularly if the target was attempting to confront the manipulator in the first place, and distracts from the issue at hand. This typically involves ad hominem arguments, meaning arguments that are meant to attack the speaker rather than disprove what is being said, denial, gas lighting, or even just speaking in circles endlessly until the point of talking about something entirely unrelated to the initial issue. All of these change the subject and focus of the conversation, keeping attention off of the manipulator if necessary, or endlessly frustrating the target to the point that the target simply gives up.

Imagine an argument between Karen and Lena. Karen is upset that Lena has accused her of shirking responsibilities and trying to get out of doing her fair share of the workload. Lena may take that accusation and run with it, pointing out the time that Karen took off work to take a sick child to the doctor, and that, had she been a better, more dedicated mother, her child never would have been sick in the first place. She may then imply that maybe CPS should be involved and that mothers have no place in the workplace, to begin with. Mothers belong at home with children so other people are not impacted by any issues that may arise with the children. If Karen was to point out that Lena has children as well, and therefore should not be welcome in the workplace either, Lena denies that that was what she said altogether.

Within this exchange, Lena has redirected the focus back onto Karen. She has said something to insult Karen directly rather than contradicting something that Karen has said, which is an ad hominem attack. Lena then denies the meaning of what was implied altogether, engaging in gas lighting, all within one argument, and suddenly, the attention has shifted from an accusation of Lena being lazy and shirking off responsibilities onto pointless bickering. Lena gets to avoid taking responsibility altogether as the initial cause of the argument goes forgotten.

Generalizing

Sometimes, manipulators seek to take a lazier route to their techniques through asserting generalizations as facts and denying anything that does not fit in. These generalizations are made to keep the manipulator from having to take the time to understand what other people are thinking or feeling. Blanket statements or generalizations can be useful tools to apply if the person generalizing is willing to entertain exceptions without entirely invalidating them, but they can also be used in manipulative ways.

Generalizations can be good, such as looking at a bear and registering all bears as dangerous. Is this true? Probably not, but it is certainly a fair and understanding assumption to come up with. On the other hand, consider creating a generalization that all female doctors are incompetent: Every time you may come across a female doctor, you assume she is incompetent with no exceptions. This is just harmful to other people, seeking to discredit people with no justification or reason.

These generalizations can be made more personal as well. Consider an argument between a husband and wife. The husband might generalize that the wife always nags, and therefore shut off his mind and tune her out any time she starts speaking in an annoyed tone. Rather than seeing what his wife may be seen as legitimate, he tells her she's always such a nag and that he does not want to hear it. On the other hand, she could tell him that he never helps her at home and that she is sick of how lazy he is. Ultimately, both the husband and the wife can either bend over backwards in an attempt to prove the generalization false, or they can allow their spouse to continue thinking the worst of them.

In manipulative situations, the manipulator may tell the other person that they are never able to do anything right in an attempt to use the blanket generalization to motivate the target into behaving in the way the manipulator wanted.

Twisting Words

Words have power. With that in mind, it makes sense, then, that twisting someone's words can allow for those words to be used against the other person. Oftentimes, manipulators will do just that. They will take what someone has said or felt and use those words or feelings against the one who has them. Typically, this involves twisting what is said to better suit the manipulator's narrative.

For example, consider a friend voicing to another she is quite unhappy with the current state of things. She may say that she wants her friend to speak more respectfully, or with fewer threats and condescending tones in her voice. Her friend may glare back and ask when the unhappy one became so perfect that she would be able to judge others. To someone watching from the outside, it is clear that the friend who complained did not say anything that attacked the other person, but the manipulative friend twisted the words around into something else. The manipulative friend may take it a few steps further asking when she had become such a bad person. The words' initial meanings were taken, misconstrued, and used to make the friend who simply wanted to be treated with respect look bad. This sort of tactic is common with manipulators, as the other person then has to backtrack, clarify how much he or she likes, respects, or loves, the manipulator, and the entire situation has been derailed.

Moving the Goalposts

Moving the goalposts is a logical fallacy. It involves constantly shifting standards so they are not attainable, giving the manipulator some way to pick at what the target has done to prove that the target is not meeting expectations. Consider an argument in which the manipulator demands that the target proves their point. Every time the target backs up his or her position, the manipulator talks about how that is not exact enough, and that it does not prove anything. To understand this, imagine the manipulator asking the target to prove that gravity exists. The target may pick up an apple or a stone and drop it on the ground, pointing to how the stone falls, calling that gravity. The manipulator may then point out how helium balloons and airplanes float, and that gravity should be holding those down, using those examples to pick at the existence of gravity. If the target points to the theory of gravity, the manipulator may pick at how that does not prove anything as it is only a theory and has not been proven without a doubt.

This can be used in interpersonal relationships as well: Consider a wife who expects her husband to bring home enough money to cater to her every whim while she sits at home. If he comes home, happy about getting a raise, she may point out that even with that raise, they still are not saving for retirement yet, and that she still has to shop using the credit card instead of paying cash. If he were to get another raise in the future that would cover those expenses as well, she would be quick to point out that they are not millionaires, so it is still not sufficient. This leaves the other person feeling incompetent and unworthy, feeling as though they are never able to live up to standards, no matter how hard they try.

Changing the Subject

Similar to the diversionary techniques in which manipulators seek to distract the target, they often will change the subject. This is often done solely to avoid responsibility, or to redirect attention to or from the manipulator. Sometimes, it happens to be the case that the manipulator can benefit from having attention turned back to him or herself, such as when discussing achievements and accomplishments. Other times, it is beneficial to shift attention away from him or herself, such as when someone is bringing up the manipulator's problematic behaviors or complaints about the manipulators.

This derailment of the conversation can lead to the original speaker's thoughts or complaints never being addressed, which is particularly useful if the manipulator is seeking to avoid being confronted or challenged. In doing so, the speaker may not remember the original complaint until after the fact, at which point, the opportunity for confrontation is entirely gone.

Threats

Oftentimes, those who manipulate will resort to threats to get what they want. They demand certain things from the people around them, and if the targets are not complying with those expectations, it is pretty stereotypical for the manipulator to resort to threats, both covert and overt. Threats are used to intimidate the other person into obedience or compliance. In response to being threatened, if the target feels as though the threat is legitimate, he or she may give in just to avoid the consequences, which is exactly what the manipulator wants.

Overt threats

Overt threats are just that. Threats that are not veiled or hidden. They are clearly threats, such as, "If you do not make sure dinner is ready when I walk in the door, every day, I will find a partner who will," "Delete all of your social media or I will leave you," or, "I will hurt you to get what I want, so you can do this the easy way or the hard way." The threat is explicitly stated to the other person, though the threat may be described in various levels of specificity, such as saying they will leave, or that they will hurt the other person, whereas others may make explicit what the intentions would be, such as whipping with a belt or getting on Tinder to meet new people.

Covert threats

While overt threats are explicit, covert threats are veiled and implied. These will be threats that are implied, but unspecified, such as, "Do what I am saying, or you will not like the consequences." This is clearly a threat, but there is nothing specific enough in it to know what may become. This could be that there is a natural consequence, such as if you do not roll up the window when it rains, your car's interior will be damaged, or it could imply that a partner will isolate, beat, or otherwise punish the person that is being threatened.

Conditioning

Conditioning takes place when manipulators teach their targets to associate them with good and all the things that make people themselves bad. For example, if Tracy is skilled at art, to the point that people actively commission her for artwork, Paul, a manipulator, may seek to get Tracy to associate that strength with negativity. He may destroy pieces of art, put down paintings, or take to screaming profanities at Tracy every time she sits down to paint or create. He seeks to make her begin to avoid art because of the association between abuse and her strengths and creativity. Instead, he will reward her any time she focuses her attention on pleasing him, eventually creating a dynamic in which she feels more comfortable and happy pleasing him instead of doing her own thing that makes her into an individual.

This is particularly insidious, as it diverts Tracy's attention and focuses away from her art and all onto Paul, corroding at things she valued, and shattering any goals of making it as a successful artist. She never gets to be a professional because he has taught her to associate it with negativity so she gives it up on her own; no longer enjoying what was once her passion due to the conditioning.

Smear Campaigns

Oftentimes, people feel as though they can avoid manipulation and abuse by never giving in to the manipulator's whims. However, when someone has resisted that, a common tactic then employed is a smear campaign, in which the manipulator seeks to ruin everyone else's opinion of the individual that got away, so to speak. The resister may not have fallen for the manipulator's antics, but everyone else did. Very quickly, that person's entire reputation is destroyed.

Even when the person is kowtowing to the manipulator's desires, the manipulator may still employ smear campaigns to ensure that the victim never has anywhere to go, should the victim decide to leave later on. It keeps the victim isolated and dependent on the manipulator. These rumors are typically false, though people somehow believe them. This is not a fault with the victim, but rather because the manipulator is simply that convincing and charismatic.

Triangulation

Triangulation involves pitting two people against each other. Typically, the manipulator will be in the ears of two different people, telling them different stories, and pitting them against each other. This creates a sort of triangle, with the manipulator at the top and the two who fall for the triangulation making the other two points, clashing with each other.

Think of a love triangle here. You have the manipulator, Martin, at the top, and his wife, Wendy, and affair partner, Ava, at the bottom two corners. Martin may be in Ava's ear, telling her how awful Wendy is and how they will soon be getting a divorce, maybe even describing how they are no longer sharing a bed and are only staying together for the remainder of the fiscal year for tax purposes. On the other hand, Martin may be telling Wendy that he loves her and that she has nothing to worry about with his coworker, Ava. The time they spend together is only platonic and professional, he may insist, despite her seeing the warning signs that her husband is cheating.

If the situation were to explode, with Ava and Wendy finally confronting each other, they would be so angry with each other, focusing on the faults with the other woman that Martin is left relatively unscathed.

Baiting

Baiting involves intentionally triggering arguments with an individual so that argument can be used against him or her. The manipulator may say something that he knows will get a rise out of the other person simply so an argument can be started and it can be used as evidence that the other person is the problem. Someone at work may make a comment, implying that a coworker does not understand and that the lack of understanding implies a lack of intelligence. This may annoy the person enough and force them to say something in response, trying to defend themselves, and ultimately, the manipulator can then instigate just enough to make the other person blow up while still retaining plausible deniability. The victim then is seen as the problem, though the victim had been baited into reacting in the first place.

Playing the Victim

Along with baiting, manipulators are skilled at playing the victim. They use this, typically in conjunction with deflecting, to twist situations in such a way that the other person is seen as the problem, even though in reality, the manipulator was the one who had caused the problem in the first place. The manipulator will never admit fault, however, and will vehemently deny any wrongdoings.

Boundary Testing

To the manipulator, boundaries are nonexistent. They are lines that are meaningless if they are not enforced, and because of that, manipulators are always testing boundaries. They respond to consequences, but if they find a weakness, they will have no qualms about completely demolishing the boundary. They want to know exactly how far they can push their targets before they incur any consequences, and the further they can push, the harder they will. This is most easily exemplified between a manipulator who often resorts to physical abuse. Every time the physical abuse occurs without consequences that are good enough deterrents from acting in a physically abusive manner, they get worse the next time. The physical abuse may start at a single slap when drunk and eventually escalate to severe beatings when entirely sober. In terms of persuasion or manipulation, a predator may test a boundary to see how much he or she can take before pushing the envelope a little further the next time. They may ask for a small favor and slowly ramp it up into expecting the targets to perform all sorts of acts and feats that are unrealistic to expect of someone else.

Hoovering

When a manipulator pushes a boundary too far and faces a consequence, they hoover their victim back in. This is a reference to the Hoover brand vacuum, directly referencing the vacuum's act of sucking back in the target that has tried to enforce the consequence. If the person left the relationship, for example, the manipulator may attempt to hoover or sweet-talk the person back with promises of doing better.

These typically are meaningless and involve saying whatever it is that the victim wants to hear in order to get him or her back in line.

Passive-Aggressive Comments and Jokes

One of the trademarks of covert narcissists, in particular, passive-aggressive jokes with a side of plausible deniability is another common manipulation tactic. Think of a mother-in-law poking her newly-postpartum daughter-in-law's stomach with a giggle and asking when the next one is due. The entire purpose of this comment, as evidenced by the mother in law's pleased expression, is to hurt her daughter-in-law by implying that she still looks pregnant, days after giving birth. If confronted, she can feign innocence, announcing that she just loves her current grandbaby so much, she cannot wait for the next one, and that it was a legitimate, innocent question. She may also spin it as a joke, along with saying that all women still look pregnant after having babies and that she is concerned that her daughter-in-law may be struggling with postpartum depression if she was hurt by what was obviously a joke. This is likely followed during the same breath with an offer to take the baby for a week while she spends time in a mental health facility.

Malignant Sarcasm

While regular sarcasm is frequently a fun, joking way to communicate or convey displeasure or annoyance when you have a rapport with the other person, it can also become a problem if the one employing sarcasm is doing it in a way that is intended to be hurtful instead of lighthearted. Manipulators may pair their sarcasm with a condescending tone, or a patronizing look similar to the one you would give a child, and their intentions under the sarcasm become obvious. They mean what they are saying and are only veiling it with sarcasm. This puts their target into a position in which they can either vocalize their dissent, in which case they are met with being told they are far too sensitive, or they can be quiet and take the hurtful comments, allowing the manipulator the satisfaction of having done exactly what was intended.

This sarcasm is frequently used in response to the target expressing thoughts. Imagine the target saying that he does not think a certain tax should be voted into law while chatting with friends, and the manipulator scoffing in response, looking at him with a smirk and announcing, "Oh, look at the politician! Where did you go to law school, huh?" Over time, similar comments or jokes about the target's thoughts and opinions leave him to the point where he feels uncomfortable voicing his own thoughts out of fear of being disparaged for them. The manipulator is able to use sarcasm to effectively silence the target into submission.

Shaming

Shaming people is another predator-favorite technique, in which the manipulator uses any of a person's sensitivities to shame the person into submission or just to hurt the victim's self-esteem because the manipulator can. While telling someone they should be ashamed of themselves is a legitimate thing to say in some instances, particularly when trying to invite self-reflection, some manipulators like to use it as a weapon.

Consider a person whose child has just passed away from cancer after a long battle and the parents eventually decided to withdraw treatment to allow their child to pass in peace, rather than painfully prolonging the child's life for selfish reasons. Someone seeking to use shame to hurt them may say, "You should be ashamed of yourself for letting that child die! That should have been declared medical neglect! Your child deserved the chance to fight!" Those exclamations are entirely intended to inflict shame, guilt, and pain on the parents, though it is undeserved and unwarranted. This erodes their self-esteem and their confidence, which is already probably at an all-time low after losing their child.

Micromanaging

The last common manipulation tactic is to micromanage in order to gain control of a situation. They seek to start small and eventually work up to controlling more and more of their victim's life. They typically begin by starting to correct or judge small decisions, purchases, or interactions, and as they are able to do that, they start to ramp it up to slightly larger ways to control other aspects of their target's life. They likely even go so far as to manipulate and micromanage their target's feelings. They may pick a fight just to put the other person in a bad mood, or downplay their target's sadness or happiness.

Chapter 4:
Neuro-Linguistic Programming (NLP)

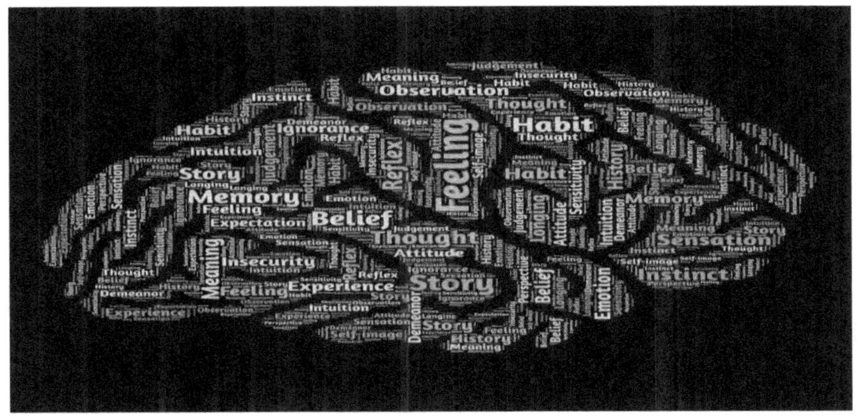

Neuro-Linguistic Programming has to do with the study of thoughts (neuro) and language (linguistic) in a systematic way and the scripts that run the life of an individual (programming).

It deals with the understanding and the development of the mind and the entire understanding of the language of the mind in relation to the way it is designed to function and how it is molded by the personal experiences of an individual. It is simply a study of a person's subjective reality.

A proper understanding of the language of the mind influences every aspect of a person's life from his relationship with others to his communication skills with friends and clients to the general outcome of a person's life. It is a holistic study that puts the spirit, body, past and present of an individual into consideration.

As Homo sapiens who are gifted with the ability to think, it is presumed that our most important function is the thought or the thinking function. NLP, however, brings one to the understanding of the fact that no thought process exists in a vacuum, as they are a product of a person's perspective. It has a presupposition of perception as reality and it holds that the things we think are colored by the way we think.

For different individuals, there are different ways of thinking and interpreting reality. What NLP does is assist in the understanding of these various representational systems to help each person narrow down his own system. It helps in the understanding of the three different types of thinking patterns which are:

- Visual - deals with both pictures and visual metaphors.
- Auditory - sound (hearing).
- Kinesthetic - deals with the five senses, as well as gut feelings.

In NLP, a person is thought to take absolute control of his mind and ultimately his life. Unlike what is obtainable in psychoanalysis, which places its focus on "why," NLP presents a more practical approach with its focus on the "how."

HOW NLP WORKS

If you are just coming across this topic for the first time, NLP may appear or seem like magic or hypnosis. When a person is undergoing therapy, this topic digs deep into the unconscious mind of the patient and filters through different layers of beliefs and the person's approach or perception of life to deduce the early childhood experiences that are responsible for a behavioral pattern.

In NLP, it is believed that everyone has the resources that are needed for positive changes in their own lives. The technique adopted here is meant to help in facilitating these changes.

Usually, when NLP is taught, it is done in a pyramidal structure. However, the most advanced techniques are left for those multi-thousand-dollar seminars. An attempt to explain this complicated subject is to state that the NLPer (as those who use NLP will often call themselves) is always paying keen attention to the person they are working on/with.

Usually, there is a large majority of NLPers that are therapists and they are very likely to be well-meaning people. They achieve their aims by paying attention to those subtle cues like the movement of the eyes, flushing of the skin, dilation of the pupil and subtle nervous tics. It is easy for an NLP user to quickly determine the following:

- The side of the brain that the person uses predominantly.
- The sense (smell, sight, etc.) that is more dominant in a person's brain.
- The way the person's brain stores and makes use of information (the NLPer can deduce all this from the person's eye movement).
- When they are telling a lie or concocting information.

When the NLP user has successfully gathered all this information, they begin to mimic the client slowly and subtly by not only taking on their body language, but also by imitating their speech and mannerisms, so that they begin to talk with the language patterns that are aimed at targeting the primary senses of the client. They will typically fake the social cues that will easily make someone let their guard down so that they become very open and suggestible.

For example, when a person's sense of sight is their most dominant sense, the NLPer will use a language that is very laden with visual metaphors to speak with them. They will say things like: "do you see what I am talking about?" or "why not look at it this way?" For a person that has a more dominant sense of hearing, he will be approached with an auditory language like: "listen to me" or "I can hear where you're coming from."

To create a rapport, the NLPer mirrors the body language and the linguistic patterns of the other person. This rapport is a mental and physiological state which a human being gets into when they lose guard of their social senses. It is done when they begin to feel like the other person who they are conversing with is just like them.

Once the NLPer has achieved this rapport, they will take charge of the interaction by leading it mildly and subtly. Thanks to the fact that they have already mirrored the other person, they will now begin to make some subtle changes in order to gain a certain influence on the behavior of the person. This is also combined with some similar subtle language patterns which lead to questions and a whole phase of some other techniques.

At this point, the NLPer will be able to tweak and twist the person to whichever direction they so desire. This only happens if the other person can't deduce that something is going on because they assume everything that is occurring is happening organically or that they have given consent to everything.

What this means is that it is quite hard to make use of NLP to get other people to act out of character, but it can be used to get a person to give responses within their normal range of character. This may come in the form of getting them to donate to a charitable cause, or finally making the decision they had been putting off or getting them to go home with you for the night if they had considered it at some previous point.

At this point, what the NLP user seeks to do may be to either elicit or anchor. When they are eliciting, they make use of both leading and language to get the person to an emotional state of say, sadness. Once they can elicit this state, they can then lead it on with a physical cue by touching the other person's shoulder for example.

According to theory, whenever the NLP user touches the person's shoulder in the same manner, the same emotional state will resurface if they do it again. However, this is only made possible by the successful conditioning of the other person.

When undergoing NLP therapy, the therapist can adopt a content-free approach, which means the therapist can work effectively without taking a critical look at the problem or without even knowing about the problem at all. This means that there is room for privacy for the client as the therapist does not need to be told about whichever event took place or whatever issue happened in the past.

Also, before the commencement of the therapy, there is an agreement which ensures that the therapist cannot disclose any information; hence the interaction between the therapist and the client remains confidential.

In NLP, there is the belief in the need for the perfection of the nature of human creation, so every client is encouraged to recognize the sensitivity of the senses and make use of them in responding to specific problems. As a matter of fact, NLP also holds the belief that the mind can find cures to diseases and sicknesses.

The techniques employed by NLP have to do with a noninvasive, medicine-free therapy that enables the client to find out new ways of handling emotional issues such as low self-esteem, lack of confidence, anxiety and destructive relationship patterns. It is also a successful tool in effective bereavement counseling.

With it's roots in the field of behavioral science, which was developed by Skinner, Pavlov and Thorndike, NLP makes use of the combination physiology and the unconscious mind to bring about change in the thought process and ultimately the behavior of a person.

THE IMPORTANCE OF NLP

Neuro-Linguistic Programming is not only necessary for the understanding of a person's being, but it also helps in the understanding of the way an individual is. It helps a person to get deep into the root cause of the problem, as well as the foundation of their being.

Here are some other reasons why NLP is important:

- It helps people take responsibility for the things that they feel they may not be able to control. With the help of NLP, a person can change the way they react to events of the past and have a certain level of control over their future.
- People need to be aware of the body language of the members of their inner circle, as well as those who they seek to do business with. With NLP, it is possible to make use of language with both control and purpose, and with this, it is possible to

have control over your life. Remember, you cannot expect to make the same mistakes using the same mindset and hope to get different results. During an NLP session, the focus is placed entirely on the client as they are made the subject. This helps a lot because, at the point where a person can deal with his or herself as a person, they gain more clarity into his or her dealings with other people.

- It helps to improve finance, sales performance, marriage, health issues, parenting, customer service and every other aspect and phase of life. This is because it helps in the holistic improvement of an individual and when a person is whole, his interactions and relationship with himself and other people become whole as well.

- It assists in targeting your beliefs, thoughts and values and helps with the targeting of a person's brain functions, as well as developing certain behaviors. It also shapes the way these behaviors metamorphoses into habits and how the habits change to actions which in turn comes as results.

NLP is applicable in different vocations and professions. This is a tool that is very important in the mastery of sales, personal development experts and self-help, teaching, communication, parenting and other facets of life.

Chapter 5:
How to Spot a Manipulator and Recognize Manipulative Behavior: Some Simple Effective Methods

Trying to figure out when somebody is taking advantage of you can be difficult. There are absolutely signs that you can watch out for. In fact, there are a lot of different great articles surrounding the thoughts of if somebody is or is not trying to take advantage of you. With the ability to see when somebody's intentions are less than pure you will keep yourself better protected and in turn, lead a happier life. It can be very frustrating when you're uncertain of someone's intentions and even worse when you find out they were simply around to take advantage of you.

People are pretty crafty, and they will use your emotions against you. Some people love to feign confusion. You may have made it very clear what your expectations are, and they simply pretend that they don't understand. If it is somebody that you know fairly well it can be easy to see that they are trying to take advantage of you because you may know that they're quite smart and usually catch on to things quickly. However, if you're dealing with somebody you don't know very well you may just assume that they're not very intelligent and need a lot of direction to get something done. Their active confusion can be frustrating and leave you dealing with whatever it was you asked of them.

DIVERT ATTENTION

When people are trying to take advantage of you, they may use diversion techniques. By throwing you off of a certain thought or path they can easily change the subject and get the eyes off of them. Being aware and staying on track of what you were saying is important. This goes hand-in-hand with knowing what you're going to say and spending the time to think before you speak. With clear concise thoughts, you won't have to worry about people trying to divert your attention away from them.

When people try to divert attention often, they are trying to pass the blame on to somebody else. This is a very dangerous game and can end up pitting you against a friend, co-worker, or family member. So, as noted it's extremely important to have your thoughts collected before entering into any sort of serious conversation. It truly can help to ensure that you do not get taken advantage of by those that are skilled and diversion techniques.

Some people will do their very best to make you feel guilty in order to be able to take advantage of you. This commonly happens with people that know you better than others. When those around you are aware of the fact that you strive to be a good person it can be used against you. There is nothing wrong with wanting to be a good person, but it does tend to make people feel guiltier when they've done something wrong.

Everyone has moments in time where they're not the best person and that's okay. Accepting the fact that everyone makes mistakes can help to ensure that those around you cannot use guilt to control you. Sure, most of us want to make good decisions and do the right thing by not only ourselves but those that are around us. Knowing that this is not always the case and we all have screw-ups is very helpful. Guilt is a common denominator and taking control over somebody or using them to your advantage.

DENIAL

Denial is another component that people frequently use to take advantage of others. If you don't have hard evidence against somebody, what is to stop them from simply saying no, I didn't do that. It then comes down to your word against theirs. If somebody is vehemently denying what you are saying eventually you start to believe it. You may question the information and where you got it. This can cause distrust among those that you trust the most.

Denial is dangerous especially when you trust your sources. Hearsay is a difficult thing to prove, however, it can be very detrimental to someone's psyche. As you start to doubt whether or not your accusations are true you may also start to doubt other things in your life. This allows control to the person that is making all of the denials. They can prey on this to try and bend you to their well. Also, once they have made you accept the fact that their denial is true, they might start looking for favors.

Neuro-linguistic programming skills can really help in this department. Most people that are quick to deny something have some facial movements or body movements to give them away. When you start to study these techniques, it can be much simpler to figure out who is riding the denial train. When you understand that somebody is simply denying the accusations to save face or keep themselves out of trouble it becomes easier to figure it out and understand that is what's going on.

LIE

Liars are all around us. From the time we were little, lying has been present in our lives, from the ones that we have told to the ones others have told us. Liars are, typically, trying to take advantage of you. Sometimes the lie that is told is quite harmless and can be brushed off. Other times, they are major lies that can ruin lives.

We talked a bit about lying earlier and when it comes down to it every person in the world tells a lie on occasion. When we tell a lie with good intent it doesn't make it much better than aligning with mal intent, but it is more understandable. Sometimes it is simply easier to tell a white lie than it is to hurt somebody's feelings or cause turmoil for somebody that you care about.

SEDUCTION

Another way in which people use to try and take advantage of others is with seduction. Let's face it; we all want to be accepted in love. Some people will use charm and flattery to get you on their side of the fence. They make you feel truly special but then end up simply getting what they want. They honestly, don't care about you one way or the other.

Recognizing when somebody is trying to seduce you can be very difficult. Obviously, if you are in a relationship and somebody is hitting on you it may be easier to blow off. Other times, when you're single and lonely, you are leaving yourself completely open to being taken advantage of. This can happen in your dating life, work-life, or even in your everyday life.

Seduction seriously plays with your emotions. Your mental stability is being challenged when you allow somebody to seduce you. Taking the time to truly get to know someone before you fall for their witty comments and compliments is crucial and keeping yourself protected against being taken advantage of.

You can ward off this kind of behavior by setting clear ground rules from the beginning. It doesn't matter if you are talking with a future lover or your boss. When people understand the ground that you keep it makes them less apt to try and take advantage of you and your emotions. Those that take advantage of your emotions are the worst as it can be very difficult to separate your rational thinking from your emotional thinking.

When you practice NLP and start to really get into the inner workings of it, it can keep you better protected from these emotional abusers. You will be able to decide whether or not somebody has the ability to affect you. Not only that, you will have the ability to decide what that effect is going to be. Having better control over yourself and your emotions is always going to help you be better protected against those who would like to play on you.

THE ART OF MINDFULNESS

A great way to add to your arsenal of maintaining control of yourself and not allowing others to take advantage or manipulate you is to practice the art of mindfulness. Mindfulness is something that we can practice every single day. There are truly some very simple exercises that can help you become more aware of what is going on around you and inside of you. Being mindful can help keep you well protected against those who wish to do you harm or have you done their bidding.

Understandably, not everybody has enough free time in a day to sit and meditate. You don't have to have a lot of time to become more mindful. It can truly only take a few minutes per day and you'll be surprised by the results. You will notice a lot more of what is happening around you and this is, obviously, advantageous to you and your overall well-being.

One exceptionally simple exercise that you can do pretty much at any point throughout your day is breathing mindfully. This means that you will change your focus from whatever it is that is in front of you and simply focus on breathing in and breathing out. Notice how it feels, the sound it makes to you, and the speed at which it is happening. The more mindful you are of your breathing the more you'll be able to focus on other things around you with continued practice.

Mindful listening is also a very easy exercise that can help to improve your senses. When you have a few minutes, you can simply close your eyes and take in, literally, every noise around you. Whether you are in the office or out for a walk in the woods the sounds will change dramatically. Hone in on each one individually; notice what the sound is, the tone of it, how it makes you feel, and how it interacts with the other sounds in the room. This practice can be done for 30 seconds or even longer. Finding the time to do it should be barely an inconvenience.

Mindful observation is a great tool to have in your kit. This is the one that is going to allow you to notice the behaviors of the people around you. By sitting back and observing what is going on without participating in it, it is surprising how many different things you will notice. We're not only talking about observing the people around you but also the surrounding itself.

Let's say you're sitting in a board meeting and you notice that the person in the corner is a little more agitated than everyone else. By looking around the room you may notice that the air is circulating to every place except for that corner. It is likely the person is feeling irritated because they're feeling heated up. This may not be something that a person would notice without practicing mindful observation.

Chapter 6:
How to Deal with a Manipulator

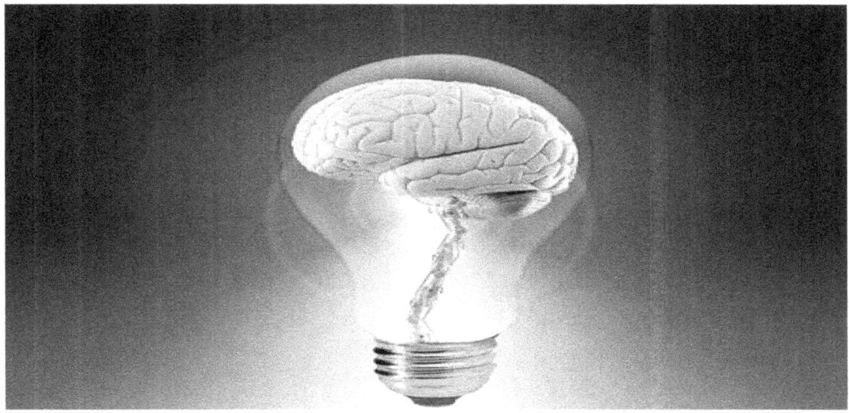

Here are some tips for dealing with manipulative people:

1. Know your fundamental rights

    The most crucial guideline when dealing with a manipulative person is to know your rights and recognize when they are being violated. As long as it seems not to hurt others, you have the right to stand up and defend our rights.

    You have the right to be treated with respect, to express your feelings and opinions, to establish your priorities, to refuse something, to have a difference of opinion, to take care of yourself, to set limits, and be happy.

2. Understand the characteristics of a manipulative person

    Observing their behaviors is essential since their manipulative tendencies are not always very obvious, however, with keen observation and some patience, their true intentions will be revealed in no time.

3. Try to change yourselves, not the manipulator

   You must focus on not being a vulnerable and easy target for a manipulator; as it is not easy for you to change them.

   However, you can change the dynamics established between the manipulator and you. Altering these dynamics causes a manipulator to stop having control and thus often they desist from their manipulative intentions.

4. Keep distance

   A way to identify a manipulator is to see if they act differently when in front of other people or in different situations. When you observe this type of behavior, the most advisable thing is to maintain a healthy distance and avoid getting involved a lot with that person. Otherwise, you can be affected.

5. Avoid making it something personal

   The manipulator seeks to exploit your weaknesses, and can make you feel inadequate or even guilty, so it's important to remember that you are not the problem nor are you to blame. Manipulators simply try to make you feel bad or guilty in order to gain more power and control over us. We must think if the other person's demands are reasonable, if we feel good about ourselves being with that person and if we are being respected.

6. Put the focus on them by asking penetrating questions

   Inevitably, psychological manipulators will request (or demand) something from you; as they often focus on satisfying their desires. Hence, you must pay attention to whether their requests are reasonable. Sometimes it may be useful to focus on them and ask them if they can recognize how unreasonable their request is. By doing this we put up a mirror to see if they can recognize their intentions and withdraw the request.

7. Take your time

Manipulators usually wait for a response immediately after asking a question and they usually exert pressure on you by reducing the time they give you to give them a response. Distancing yourself from the influence of the manipulator by thinking before answering usually helps you make better decisions since you will be able to evaluate the pros and cons with greater tranquility.

8. Learn to say "No" diplomatically

Communicating assertively allows you to express your desires more easily without your decisions being violated. You should not be afraid of refusing something or feel guilty for not satisfying someone else's demands.

9. Confront

In order to keep you passive and docile, a manipulator might try to influence you strongly because they think you are weak. However, you need to portray yourself as a strong individual capable of defending your rights.

Confronting someone puts you in a safe position and makes you feel less vulnerable. Also, confronting a manipulator would make them see that you're aware of their purpose and that their manipulation strategies are not going unnoticed.

Chapter 7: Brainwashing

Brainwashing as a manipulation technique is far more powerful than both mind control and hypnosis, but it also requires far more training and expertise to be used most efficiently. While many of the concepts used in hypnosis and mind control overlap with brainwashing, there are also new techniques made available to you when you learn about brainwashing. Like hypnosis, brainwashing is a popular topic and plot device in many books, movies, and other media. Of course, as well as being the most powerful technique, brainwashing is also more high-profile than hypnosis and mind control. It has been used extensively in certain large-scale scenarios, including by certain governments, cults, corporations, etc. While brainwashing has been known throughout history by many different names, including thought reform, thought control, coercive persuasion, and re-education for the sake of simplicity, this will only refer to it as brainwashing.

By learning more about what brainwashing is and how it works, you will not only have gained a valuable technique for manipulating other people, but you will also be able to more easily recognize when you are being brainwashed by another person or by an organization.

The History of Brainwashing

One of the most well-known portrayals of brainwashing on a massive scale in fiction is found in the book 1984, which was written by George Orwell in 1949. In the book, a massive government entity maintains complete control over its citizens by creating propaganda, using surveillance to spy on people, rationing food, and even training people to use a different language.

There is no magical technology that allows the government to directly control its citizens' thoughts and actions. Still, through the laws it creates and how it enforces those laws, it can make its citizens think and act in only the ways that it wants them to.

Even though 1984 is a work of fiction, governments like the one described in the book have certainly existed in real life and continue to do so today. Of course, brainwashing has been used by other organizations than governments in its history, and different groups have used brainwashing successfully in different ways to further their goals.

While certain forms of brainwashing techniques have been in use for thousands of years, the public did not become aware of brainwashing on a large scale until the 1940s and the 1950s.

At that time, brainwashing was a major part of society in China under Mao Zedong, the Chairman of the Communist Party of China and China's leader overall. The term "brainwashing" comes from the Chinese phrase "xǐnǎo", which translates to "wash brain" in English. Americans were not made aware of brainwashing as a phenomenon until after the Korean War had begun. During the war, American soldiers were captured as prisoners of war (POWs), and during their time spent in Chinese prison facilities, they were brainwashed by the Chinese government. The POWs that had been brainwashed were more likely to give over classified information to the Chinese and give false confessions, more willing to do what their captors wanted them to, and even defended the Chinese government's actions.

The United Nations commander at the time stated that "too familiar are the mind-annihilating methods of these Communists in forcing whatever words they want. The men themselves are not to be liable and they have my deepest compassion for having been used in this awful way." In other words, the Chinese were extremely skilled at brainwashing their victims, who would feel the effects of being brainwashed for years after it had been done to them. After American POWs were found to have been brainwashed, the United States Central Intelligence Agency (CIA) ran a series of experiments over twenty years that tested mind control and brainwashing capabilities, the most famous of these experiments being called Project MKUltra. To test general brainwashing techniques, the CIA also experimented with drugs as a tool for manipulation and attempted to create a so-called truth serum that would be used for interrogation purposes.

From there, brainwashing took hold in the public's minds and began to play a large part in popular culture. Large audiences received stories involving brainwashing, and movies such as The Fear makers, Toward the Unknown, The Bamboo Prison, The Rack, and The Manchurian Candidate were all inspired in some part by the experience of American POWs during the war or brainwashing in general. Starting in the late 1960s and extending through the mid-1970s, brainwashing as a concept was so deeply rooted in the public consciousness that it even seeped into the criminal justice system. Perhaps the most famous example is Patty Hearst, an heiress who was kidnapped and brainwashed by a terrorist group known as the Symbionese Liberation Army (SLA). She later joined the group as a member and was arrested during an attempted bank robbery.

Her trial was the first widely publicized instance of using brainwashing as a legal defense in court. While she was ultimately found guilty, the defense caused a renewal of interest and concern over brainwashing.

Since the 1960s, brainwashing has also been widely used in recruiting members to cults. The most well-known instance of brainwashing being used in cults is probably that of the Manson Family, founded in 1967 by Charles Manson. Manson was an extremely skilled manipulator, and successfully recruited nearly 100 people, mostly women, into his cult following. He had such a strong influence over them that he was able to convince them to commit several different crimes, from assault and robbery to mass murder. Nearly all cults use some form of brainwashing to influence potential recruits and convince them to join, from the most infamous to cults you have never heard of before. Some cults, such as Heaven's Gate and The People's Temple, used brainwashing to such a powerful effect that their followers were convinced to commit suicide.

Cults are especially important to study brainwashing because they demonstrate how far the power of brainwashing techniques can take people and are a good indicator of when things have gone too far. Suppose you are thinking of using brainwashing or any other manipulation on a person to make them inflict harm on themselves or anyone else. In that case, you should refrain from doing so and seek professional help for yourself.

But why is the history of brainwashing so important to learn about? After all, you are not a government entity such as the Communist Party of China, and you are hopefully not planning on dabbling in becoming a cult leader of any kind. Of course, there are valuable lessons to be learned from the history of brainwashing that you can apply to how you approach and implement brainwashing techniques in your own life. First of all, having a great understanding of brainwashing history should mean that you also have a good understanding of just how powerful brainwashing can be, even on the most unwilling targets. If American soldiers can be brainwashed into defending their captors, the country's enemies that they vowed to serve, then imagine what brainwashing can do for you if used correctly. Secondly, brainwashing history teaches the important lesson that anybody and everybody is susceptible to brainwashing techniques unlike mind control and hypnosis. If you focus on honing your talents and become a skilled enough manipulator, you can brainwash not just one person, but multiple people at a time into doing whatever it is that you want for them to do. The most talented manipulators can exert their influence over hundreds of people all at once, and every single one of their targets will be as thoroughly taught as the last one. This leads me into the final reason why the history of brainwashing is important to have at least some knowledge of because brainwashing is such a powerful and effective tool that can be used on so many people, it can be easy to take brainwashing too far, and force your targets into criminal or even life-threatening situations. By studying brainwashing history, you will know how horrible the effects of brainwashing can be for the target, the manipulator, and for anybody else who gets caught in between. While brainwashing as a tactic is not in and of itself harmful, when used with reckless abandon, things can quickly spiral out of control. As the manipulator, it is your responsibility to know when to stop before something terrible has occurred. Above all else, brainwashing history demonstrates the need to be safe, sensible, and responsible when using brainwashing techniques, as the consequences can be dire if brainwashing is used irresponsibly.

10 STEPS OF BRAINWASHING

Brainwashing phrases are mostly separate and can be generally divided into three levels. The first stage involves all the methods the abuser takes to tear down their prey; the second phase requires convincing the prey that there is a possibility of redemption; and lastly, the 3rd stage involves guiding the survivor to heaven most their idea of redemption.

First Stage: Breaking the Target

Step 1: Identity Assaulting

To break down a predator's target, they may be the first target that makes the victim what they are: their ego or identity. Each human being has in his mind an idea of himself which is what they claim to be. This is the way they define themselves. Multiple identities are possible. You could be a mother and a career woman. You may be a smart businessman and an uncle. You may be a hard-fought student at the class. You just might be a Christian. You can choose between endless identities. That identity is your solution to the declaration "tell me about yourself a little bit".

Suppose one day you wake up and someone advises you that you're not really what you believe you are. How do you manage to hear that? If this was deliberated in passing, you should possibly shrug it off and go on with your career. Or maybe you'd worry about it for a few hours or minutes, and maybe get frustrated for a bit, then push on. Now imagine someone comes to your home every minute of the day to remind you that you're not the guy you believe you are. How'd that help you feel? If it lasted through months or even weeks, then you will be out of your head by the end of it. You will be startled and left to question where to distinguish between fiction and fact.

If you'd thought about yourself as a great writer before, you'd start to doubt it. If you thought you were your children's biological father, you may start questioning him. If you've grown up thinking you're a real catholic, hearing daily contradictory reports would make you start thinking you might not be.

The first phase in the brainwashing cycle is when the entire dirty work starts taking hold. An individual who has planted the ugly seed of doubt in them is endangered to manipulation. We want to think the best of ourselves, as human beings. Also, we like having other people believe in us the best. Yes, some individuals may not care about someone else's validation and approval. That's admirable and we should all be working towards that. But at the end of the day, the guy who goes to bed thinking he is the worst sleeps more restlessly. Having high self-esteem and a strong sense of self, of course, saves you from the predators willing to attack you.

The result of the first phase of brainwashing is a completely-blown identity issue which the predator could prey on for the second step's purposes.

Step 2: Guilt Manipulation

Guilt, as it's been called, maybe a negative emotion, it is also a quite strong feeling. Guilt can start making you, as a person, promise things outside of your scope. Guilt will make you sit awake for hours wondering if you're such a bad human being because you're not. The human creatures around us are continually harnessing the strength of liability.

This is how the second phase of brainwashing tends to work: a brainwasher has indeed convinced its victim that they're not really what they've always assumed to be. Hence, the survivor is in a state of uncertainty because they try to address the issue of identification. So, if they aren't a decent person, what are they then? The predator glides in at this point and begins to take them for their lives' entire sorrow trip. When you're uncertain who you are, it can be tempting to accept every falsehood you're getting fed up with about you. A brainwasher would also make a statement convincing their perpetrator that they are a nasty friend, irrespective of how this adverb is being used.

Steps 3 and 4: Personality-betrayal and breaking point

Even citizens themselves are intensely loyal. They're going to protect themselves and their behavior, and struggle to hear their words. Particularly the individuals who are afraid of speaking up for anyone also will speak up for themselves. A person having been brainwashed is the total opposite. Brainwashed people have no trouble rejecting themselves and anything else connected to them despite being continuously bombarded by signals about being the reverse about what they once considered themselves to be. This involves their family, associates, value framework, and all other relationships they might have that link them to the old identification that has been 'evaluated' by the brainwasher and found 'seriously missing.'

There are several reasons why a person who has been brainwashed can easily find himself in this step and cannot fight back. For beginners, they've already moved through the first 2 phases and come out in doubt and guilt, feeling drowning and disoriented. But frequently they don't have the strength to strike off. Remember that there is sometimes a risk of serious harm if conformance is not accomplished, so the goal may be too scared to contradict all the predator's replies.

Second Stage: Dangling a Salvation Carrot

Step 5: The Olive Branch

After the first 3 stages of brainwashing, a survivor of brainwashing sometimes feels so bad about themselves because they try to save themselves at whatever expense. The survivor is also in bad emotional health and has a weak self-image. Those who have forgotten their longtime sense of belonging and will clutch up on any straws offered to feel something again. At this stage, a victim becomes expected to experience a nervous collapse, and that is the signal for the attacker to leap in and deliver redemption.

The manipulator would offer an olive branch after tearing down their objective for a long period so that the goal will slip into the pit of thinking there is hope at the end of a tunnel. An olive branch at this point could be something from a sweet word to a gift, or perhaps even some type of personal affection. This olive branch helps to demonstrate the goal that there is certain leniency to gain when they're on the right side of the manipulator. A manipulator is above all a 'normal guy' who wishes them the best. That is at least what they have learned since the start of brainwashing.

Step 6: Being Forced to Confess

Take into account: You have been confined for an amount of time to intense mental abuse by an individual. You have wasted your sense of belonging and feel confused and angry. You're facing a psychotic collapse or already experienced one and can't make every part of your life head or tails. Since leaving the social network you have existed in solitary isolation and can't think of the last moment you had such a decent meal. Then, one day, this individual comes up at your door carrying a steaming coffee pot and freshly prepared muffins. They just say they want to chat. You are inviting them to your building. You just can't believe it. It's the only love you've been receiving in the longest period. What do you believe your former abuser will be reacting to this unusual kindness?

You'll experience a sense of sovereign debt more often than not. Human beings enjoy being kind enough to reciprocate that compassion. Whenever somebody does something good for you, it is only natural to want to do something even better for them. For a brainwashed human, the desire to repay a kindness is far much greater as they believe they still have to compensate for anything they are incorrect about. The brainwashed side, therefore, will be more than willing to offer away some type of kindness. This goodness would always come in the shape of a lie, in their troubled minds. The perpetrator would usually give the alternative of an apology as a means to get paid back.

Step 7: Guilt Channeling

A brainwashed survivor is frequently filled with so much crushing remorse that they still have no scope for any other feeling after weeks or months of being told they're mistaken on everything. The goal has been swamped by so much abuser psychological torment they don't even realize what makes them feel bad anymore. The victim simply knows he's guilty of anything. In this misunderstanding, the manipulator glides in and persuades them that guilt is due to all the bad people they've believed in before. The predator, in other words, streams the guilt into the system of belief. The victim now begins to associate their beliefs with the guilt and the responsibility of dealing with the guilt. By fact, the abuser wants to help their prey continue to equate all the negative emotions of their history and let them think that if they select different values, there is a possibility to be rescued and feel stronger.

Step 8: Guilt Relief

The victim is beginning to feel a little relieved to recognize that he's just not deeply bad; perhaps, it is his perceptions that are wrong. He can be correct again, by detaching himself from his beliefs. He sheds his remorse by relinquishing anything related to his prejudices, even those nearest to him. He admits the mistakes of his previous ways and can embark on the current set of values that the brainwasher provides.

Third Stage: Reconstruction of a Brainwashed Self

Step 9: Harmony and Progress

At this stage in brainwashing, the target is keen to redeem itself and look very good in the brainwasher's eyes. Even so, they will start rebuilding a new identity based on the manipulator's offered belief system. After passing through the torture and suffering of the early phases of brainwashing, an offender is assured that only pain and guilt will come from their old belief system. They are glad to be rid of the former life and replaced with a new self that is their safe place from all their suffering.

Step 10: Rebirth and Final Confession

The survivor also experiences a sense of satisfaction upon embracing the current moral structure to be finished for their history and all of the resulting pain. Like the stereotypical last rope on a sinking ship, they must stick to their new identities as this is the only happiness they have experienced in a long period. At this stage, the brainwasher succeeded in obtaining a conversion, and might even be conducting a ritual to invite the latest conversion into the holy inner circle. It is typical for the majority of offenders to be separated from their families. They're going to get it in their heads that they're better individuals today and don't have to deal with their previous negative stuff.

Chapter 8:
The Art of Speed Reading People

Speed reading is one of the most popular and powerful methods used to identify differences in people. It is used to gain an in-depth understanding of people types and how this affects their behavior.

Speed reading utilizes several proven techniques to help you understand other people's motivations and emotions so that you can customize your approach to them for a more effective impact. In simple terms, speed-reading refers to the ability to read other people quickly and using this to influence their decisions and abilities. Speed-reading involves reading a person's body language signals. The difference between this and other types of people reading is that speed-reading does not involve the study of hundreds of nonverbal signals. Instead, the reader uses some form of intuition to gain information about others.

To be effective in speed-reading, it is advised that you focus on big signals, not the small ones. This technique involves concentrating on the other person and knowing when to trigger a conversation with them. These conversations will sometimes go well but flop at other times. As you converse with people, you must be quick enough to grasp some of your mind's evident signals to process.

The essence of speed-reading is to eliminate the struggle people go through to capture every signal sent by others. When you spend a lot of time trying to process these signals, the conversation may end as soon as it begins. It is not easy to be talking to someone while your mind is busy processing every kind of movement that the person makes. Doing this eliminates the possibility of identifying exactly what the person is thinking or feeling. To keep it simple, try applying the technique of speed-reading. Focus on the big movements and ignore the small ones.

For instance, a person who is bored with the conversation will always withdraw eye contact or turn to face the opposite direction. Smiling or nodding of the head automatically shows you that the person is happy. When it comes to speed reading, you should not waste your time trying to unlock the meaning of things you do not understand. When you do this, you may end up with the wrong interpretation of the person, resulting in the wrong judgment.

Speed Reading and the Law of Reverse Effect

Speed-reading is something that is done by the subconscious mind. Forcing your conscious mind to perform this duty results in what is known as the law of reverse effect. When looking for information to read from the other person, you may once in a while overthink some signals and start processing them beyond the subconscious mind. This can make you appear too distant from the conversation. The best way to avoid this is by allowing your unconscious mind to do all the processing. Trust your intuitions and gut instincts. This will help you to understand some signals without having to think deeply about their meaning.

Instincts are derived from real science. It is believed that some of the hollow organs of the body, like intestines, contain nerves that act as a secondary brain that transmits signals to the main brain. This is why a person's intuition is often referred to as his 'gut instincts.' Intuition is a way of the mind indicating that it already has received some information about the situation at hand.

Another important aspect of speed-reading is the ability to remain calm during times of discomfort. This is one of the easiest ways that boost your ability to speed read other people. When you are at peace, it is easier to relax during weird circumstances, and this means that you will be able to handle any tension that arises when things get tough. One way to achieve this is through mindful breathing. You can do this by concentrating on certain simple exercises that help you slowly breathe in via your nose and breathe out through the mouth. This helps you to relax your panic muscles as you continue to read others.

Speed Reading and Receptiveness

Some people often try as much as possible not to send any non-verbal signals to others. Most salespeople and those whose roles involve negotiation often do this. You can get these people to reveal their true thoughts and feelings by doing something they least expect from you. This will cause them to be distracted, and as a result, they will display some genuine reactions. For instance, you can tease them in a friendly manner, or ask rhetorical questions that will stir their emotions at once.

You may also decide to use what is known as provocative therapy. This involves an act of trying to convince them otherwise or by bluffing them. This will confuse the person who will then reveal his true identity. Practicing these strategies while remaining focused can help you grow faster to become an expert in speed-reading.

Several guidelines apply when it comes to speed-reading; these are:

- Adopting the best approach – just like we said earlier, do not get distracted trying to read every signal sent your way. Also, you should avoid thinking ahead of what is happening at the moment. The process of speed-reading involves specifying exactly what you want to know from a person and concentrating on it.
- Monitor your Eye Movement – control the way you move your eyes. This is because the other person may also be skilled in seed reading and therefore, they might get the wrong signal just by observing your eye movement

- Maintain a certain pattern – speed-reading needs a sense of pattern or rhythm. Assess the person one trait or signal at a time. You may make a pre-list of the things you wish to find out and use this list to analyze the person. Avoid revisiting old signals and concentrate on learning something new, unless if it is necessary

- Process ideas, not words – when interacting with others, do not focus more on the words but the words' signals. The faster you read someone, the better for you since some people tend to hide their real emotions as the conversation continues. Seek knowledge about some of the signals that other people send. This will speed up the process of visualizing meaning from other people's reactions. As a result, reading sessions will be made shorter and more effective.

- Suppress your bad habits – human behavior is made of a collection of habits. It is ideal that when speed reading, you identify some of the bad habits you have and slowly work on minimizing them.

Speed-reading other people has a good number of benefits. One of them is that the technique trains your mind to become more focused, thus improving its processing capacity and capability. It also gives you a better understanding of others, and this influences how you treat them in the future. Speed-reading always flexes the brain and exercises brain muscles. This translates to better memory retention, and as a result, you will be able to become more alert during speed-reading sessions.

As you speed-read others, you may identify some information and traits that will improve your personality. Once you master the art of speed-reading, you will always appear more confident when with your peers, who will also see you as an emotionally intelligent person. You may also identify several new opportunities as you speed-read people. This is because most of them will trust your abilities and may recommend some good opportunities. Your ability to grasp things quickly will always act as a plus, and you will easily assimilate data, which you can then use to innovate new strategies and ideas. Once you master the art of speed-reading, your confidence may pave the way for leadership positions, and this will result in better earnings in terms of salaries and allowances.

In conclusion, learning how to speed read requires a lot of patience. You must be a person that grasps processes and information easily. Even without a real speed reading session, you must be able to practice this technique frequently to become better at it.

Chapter 9:
Verbal and Non-Verbal Cues

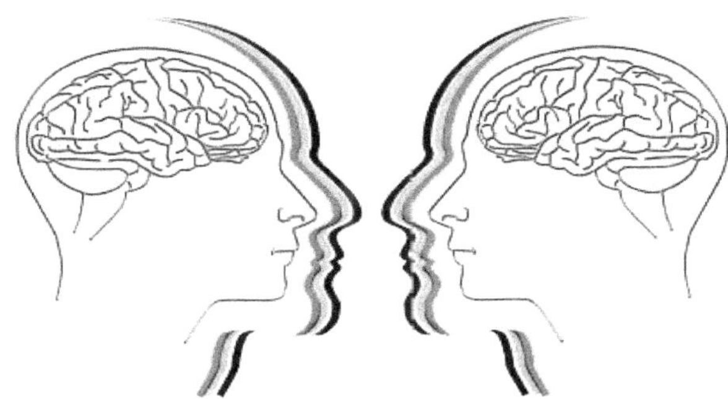

Naturally, you can tell a lot about a person by what they say. You can also tell a lot by what they don't say. Verbal and non-verbal cues are two powerful ways that you can get into the mind of someone else to truly understand them. The best manipulators are masters at reading what someone is saying (and not saying) to quickly analyze what drives them and what they are thinking.

Many cues are held in verbal language. To study verbal and non-verbal cues in-depth would take at least one, if not several books to get a strong idea of exactly what every verbal and non-verbal cue means. For that reason, we are simply going to analyze common phrases and what they mean. This will help you generate an understanding of the tone of voice and words themselves, allowing you to customize this skill to anything your subject is saying to you. In most cases, the cues remain the same even if the sentence structure varies slightly.

"I was on another television show last night."

The operative term in a sentence like this is "another". This person has not only done something multiple times, in this case appearing on TV, but they also need to make sure other people know about it, too. They are often doing this to boost their social class and improve their self-image in front of their peers. If they brag by saying words such as "another", "again" or other similar words, they are trying to make their bragging look casual, as if they are completely used to that experience and it is normal for them. The implied reasoning is that they are of a higher social status than they may actually feel that they are.

"I worked hard to get to where I am today."

The operative term in this sentence is "hard". Someone who says something such as "I worked hard" or "It was hard" believes that they are not worthy of their achievements. Instead, they believe that they would have never gotten there had they not exerted themselves and worked as hard as they possibly could to get there. They are often proud of their accomplishments but may struggle with self-esteem issues.

"I waited patiently for her to finish before I left."

The operative word here is "patiently". This person is implying that they wanted to get out of said place or that they were in a rush, but that they were willing to wait for something to be completed, for example, someone speaking. This means that even when they are in a rush or they have prior commitments, they are committed to seeing things through. They have personal restraint and are willing to settle down and hold back so that they don't upset anyone or cause a scene where one is not needed. They may also be somewhat complacent and willing to let people get away with things for fear of standing up for themselves.

"I decided to buy the top."

Here, the operative word is "decided". In this case, the person decided to purchase the top. This means that they had to think about whether they actually wanted it or not. They put thought into the process before actually following through. The alternative would be a phrase like "I just bought that top". Here, "just" would imply that they purchased it impulsively without thinking about it.

"It was the right thing to do."

Here, the person is emphasizing on the topic being "right". They were struggling with a moral or potentially legal or ethical dilemma. They struggled to make the right decision, likely because it was hard for them. Still, they did it. This shows that the person has the ability to be fair and do the right thing, no matter how hard it is. People like this are often very considerate toward others and want to make sure that everyone involved is happy and treated fairly.

Chapter 10: Body Language and How to Analyze It

Body language, also called non-verbal language, can be defined as an external reflection of a person's emotional condition. This reflection is manifested through the use of non-verbal messages that can be universal or specific to a specific geographical area or culture, but in any case, they have a very specific meaning that serves to express a feeling, a thought or a state of mind. Every movement and gesture is an indicator of some emotion that an individual feel at a certain moment.

When is a non-verbal language used?

We can safely answer "always!"

Nonverbal expressions and gestures go hand in hand with the words spoken, but also when we do not speak because, for example, when we have to be silent in a library and therefore we express ourselves by gestures or while we are in a place where there is particularly noise and we gesticulate to make ourselves understood.

Non-verbal language is used when speaking with a person, with a group of people or while using a telephone even if you are fully aware that they cannot see us on the other side of the telephone. Non-verbal communication is something that's unconscious; body language starts up unconsciously, with or without words, and communicates the real feelings and sensations of who is speaking to you.

The key to reading body language well is also being able to understand a person's emotional conditions by paying attention both to their verbal communication and to everything they transmit with non-verbal language, knowingly or unknowingly, and identifying the situation in which they are expressing themselves. This allows you to distinguish truth from imagination and reality from fantasy.

We assume that the key to reading body language is not a simple thing but it can become easy, strangely many people believe that doing this is a very difficult thing. This is because many know nothing about body language. Knowing little or nothing about something we need to do, and if we don't put in even a minimum of effort to try to find a solution, then it is logical that we will never succeed in what we are doing. This applies to any concept, even to body language.

The struggle lies in the fact that these movements are numerous, very fast and tend to have different meanings. To facilitate their understanding, scholars have divided them into various groups and subgroups, according to which part of the body is affected by the movement.

Many times what a person says when he is speaking to us does not correspond with the gestures of his body, it becomes indispensable to be able to decipher these movements, because this discrepancy is an indication of lies. To do this one must first be able to recognize these gestures and then be able to attribute the right meaning to them.

When we humans say that a person is intuitive or perceptive to others, we refer to the ability to read the various body languages of others and compare the signals with the words they pronounce. Being able to do this puts us in a position to understand the true intentions of those around us and to anticipate their actions, both for better and for worse. Some people manage to do it automatically and are unaware; others need to work on it a bit.

This is also what is called public awareness or relationships with a group. It is the ability of a person to quickly understand if the person or audience he is addressing is interested and attentive to what he says. For example, if a certain audience is comfortably relaxing with their arms crossed and their chin lowered, then the speaker who is giving the speech will realize that perhaps he is not expressing himself in the best way, but above all, he is not using the language of the body in the best way. He will therefore have to take a different approach to be able to get the audience involved.

If, on the other hand, the speaker continues to speak in the same way without doing anything to attract the attention of the audience, it means that he does not have great speaking skills and will not be able to convey his message and therefore his ideas and opinions. If during a speech this happens and that is that the attention of the public is lacking it means that the speaker certainly has gaps in the knowledge and management of body language, otherwise he would not have reached that point. A good knowledge and mastery of body language often lead you to have excellent results in the field of communication and to be more intuitive, as this knowledge can be applied to others who interact with you.

In general, women are much more intuitive than men, and this is what led to the term "intuition of women" that people commonly use in stories about women. Women are fortunate to have, in most cases, an innate ability to decipher non-verbal cues and to have an impeccable eye for small details. This is one of the reasons why very few husbands can lie to their wives and get away with it. It is also the reason why women can, on the contrary, pull the wool over a man's eyes without the man noticing.

Research conducted by psychologists from Harvard University has established that women are much more attentive to body language than men. They showed short films while the sounds were turned off. The films consisted of a woman and a man in a conversation. Participants were then asked to decode what was happening by reading the couples' expressions. According to the research, women have been able to read the situation accurately 87% of the time, while men have just achieved a 42% accuracy score. Men, who are cultivating from professions of the artistic nature, have done almost as much as women. Gays, on the other hand, also scored quite well. The ability of women to be more intuitive than men has been studied and is connected to the fact that it is precisely the woman who has to take care of her offspring from the first day of life from breastfeeding to weaning in particular, to develop skills that will be useful for deciphering and understanding everything that happens in her immediate neighbor just to be able to protect her children. These innate abilities have adapted to our daily, social and professional life in the course of evolution; which is why females are often more intuitive negotiators than males because they tend to practice reading signals in advance. Body language is an instrument that is used practically throughout the day, every day and three hundred sixty-five days a year, it is used with animals, regardless of your mood, whether you are alone or you have some company, at home or at work, with your partner or with your employer, with children or with the elderly.

Body language can be defined as open, if it involves opening gestures that tend to be expansive, such as the gesture that involves bringing the palms up or showing them and keeping them well in sight. This is a clear sign of openness and that is usually done automatically when you want to convey a sense of honesty, truth and clarity.

The greatest difficulty when talking about body language is represented by errors in the interpretation of gestures. This is because you may happen to see very similar movements, such as shrugs, and make the mistake of attributing the same meaning to everyone. Nothing more wrong! For example, if today you ask John if he knows where his friend Mark has parked the car and he says no and in the meantime, he shrugs both shoulders at the same time and prolongs the movement for a few seconds, then it means that he doesn't really know. If instead you ask Paul what happened between Mark and Sam and he replies that he does not know but wants information about it, while he says this he only raises a shoulder for a fraction of a second and then lowers it immediately then he is lying because his movement shows disinterest.

Another gesture that we can find several times even on the same day is the smile on a person's face. The smile indicates a positive emotion, expresses a positive feeling. So are all the people we meet who smile really happy? And here the donkey falls! Oh yes, because it has been shown by several studies that individuals not only manage to smile in a piloted way, but they also manage to do it in a very convincing way especially when they want to hide a disappointment or something they don't like. This is the case of the classic fake smile or also called "Duchenne smile" from the name of the scholar who discovered and analyzed it. The difference between a true and a false smile is that the first one involves almost all the facial muscles and causes the so-called "crow's feet" wrinkles around the eyes, an irrefutable sign, while the second does not.

Have you noticed that just introducing the topic of body language, starting only to define it, a range of options and facets applicable to daily life has opened up? And we have not yet started talking specifically about the various types of body language and the movements of each of them!

You have already noticed, making only a few examples, as it is evident that some things we already know, some small gestures that we have seen thousands of times done or that we have even done thousands and thousands of times but without taking them into consideration much, can have important meanings and can they give us the solution to understand many things that we didn't even notice before? In the following pages, we will analyze most of the gestures that are part of body language and for convenience, I will divide them into categories and sub-categories in order to simplify and speed up their learning as much as possible.

We can therefore divide body language into three main major groups:

- The language of the head, which includes facial expressions and movements of the whole face;
- The language of the trunk, which includes the gestures of hands and arms and the movements or positions that the trunk assumes;

- The language of the lower body, which includes the movements of the legs and feet and how they can be positioned.

Also, three very important factors affect each of the body languages and are:

- Posture, which indicates the position that an individual assumes with his body;
- Proxemics, i.e. the social distance between individuals;
- Physical contact during a conversation. Posture is the fundamental component that most influences body language because it is as if it were a person's business card.

It is the initial thing you notice when you meet someone before you even notice the color of the eyes, the shape of the lips or any other type of body movement. Do you think all this material is enough to start taking your first steps in the world of body language? I think so! Now let's start analyzing one topic at a time.

Chapter 11:
Understanding the People Around You

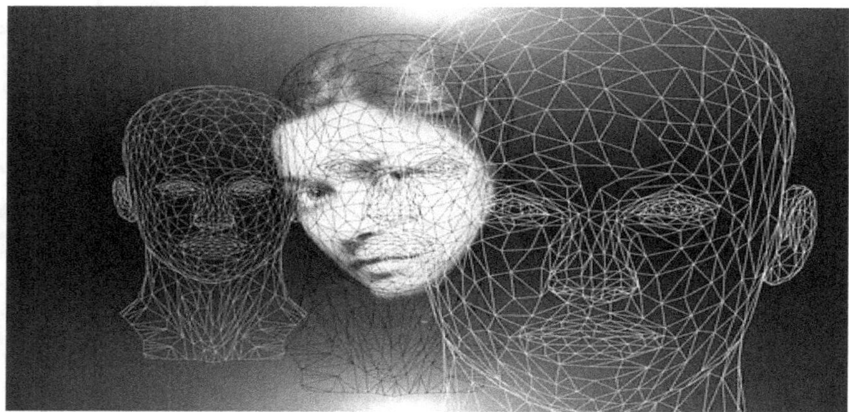

You've arrived at the point where we start to get technical and learn the meaning behind body movement so you can start putting to work everything you've learned about reading people. I want to make sure this chapter goes deep enough and addresses all the significant areas of the body that you need to learn to interpret.

THE FACE

Our face continually transmits information, whether we know it or not. Think of it more like a projector sharing with the world what's going on, on the inside. But there are many myths around what a face is saying that you need to become aware of to avoid misinterpretation.

Depending on one's ethnic or cultural background (and at times, it may also be that someone is introverted or extroverted), their facial expression may or may not be easily understood by you. I want you to avoid miscommunication. To do that, you need to look deeper than just commonly promoted ideas. For example, all our faces are coated with numerous creases and lines along with varying degrees of thickness. So that means a person's face is always transmitting some information. But are you able to skillfully figure out what that information is?

Common sense dictates that when a person is relaxed, their facial muscles will also be relaxed. The opposite is also true. And suppose you're speaking with someone who seems to convey a compelling emotional message verbally, yet looking at his or her facial expression, not much intensity is demonstrated. What does that tell you? Perhaps the person isn't as emotionally stimulated as they want you to believe. Of course, the more you know this person and understand their baseline behavior, the easier it can be to notice this difference. The primary emotions we tend to express frequently through our facial expressions include happiness, sadness, anger, surprise, disgust, fear, confusion, excitement, desire, and contempt.

Facial expressions, although a double-edged sword depending on how we use them, make it easy to read body language. You can spot a happy face, sad face, depressed face, or angry face a mile away. The lesson for you, in this case, isn't about learning to spot and read faces, but instead, it's about giving digging deeper to uncover some of the hidden messages that often go unnoticed. Many people have learned to mask their emotions. They might be "faking a smile" or pretending to be interested in you. In such cases, you need to know how to detect their micro-expressions. Whenever someone is showing an expression that contradicts what they are feeling inside, you will catch a glimpse of their real expression in an instant as they attempt to control their body language. Usually, these facial expressions only last a split second, and although hard to catch, it's good to start looking out for them whenever you interact with someone.

Eyes and Eyebrows

We often hear the eyes are the windows to the soul. But how much of the information around reading eye movement is accurately representative of the truth? There are a lot of myths around the eyes that we need to address first. For a long time, it was believed that an honest person always looks you in the eye, and so when someone doesn't, it was considered a sign of deception. That is one of the many myths you need to become aware of. Every culture carries its own tradition around how much eye contact is acceptable. So if you're talking to someone and they don't start you straight in the eye, don't be so quick to judge. Instead of getting biased, use these standard signals to try and pick up what the person is communicating.

Notice The Pupil.

When someone is excited about something, the natural reaction of the pupil is to dilate. The opposite is also true. If the person is angry or offended for some reason, the pupil will automatically contract. Taking notice of the size of the pupil and the different changes that occur as you interact with them can help you get a sense of how the other person is receiving the communication and whether or not you are keeping their attention.

The Eyebrows

Aside from the eyes and the pupil, your eyebrows or that of a counterpart also expresses feelings. For example, in women, raised eyebrows are indicative of friendless and sometimes even submissiveness. With the overabundance of selfies on social media today, I encourage you to find selfies of people who are showing off their faces. Notice that you'll tend to feel more attractive to a particular "look," and more often than not, if you dig deep, it will have a lot to do with the eyes and the eyebrows. Raised eyebrows and lowered eyelids come across as very attractive and suggestive. It's not threatening. But lowered eyebrows give off a mean authoritative look. They tend to communicate dominance and aggression. Combine lowered eyebrows with glaring eyes, and no one will want to hang around you!

How to Read People Using 'the Eyes'.

The first step is to figure out someone's baseline. Everyone will have their baseline, i.e., how they act under normal, non-threatening conditions. That means you need to invest some time with the person you want to read and casually engage in neutral topics that they would have no reason to get defensive or lie about. Daily mundane things like the weather are a great starting point. Once you understand the baseline, it's easy to spot the clues that let you know something is off. Some of these clues include:

Squinting - this often occurs when someone doesn't like you or what you're saying. It can indicate suspicion unless it's a dimly lit environment in which case they might be attempting to see more clearly. If someone squints at you, take a moment to address him or her directly and clarify your statement.

Eye blocking - this often occurs in the form of covering or shielding. You can also see a lot of blinking or eye rubbing. It's a powerful display of disagreement, disbelief, or fear.

Eye direction - several studies say when someone looks up to the right, they are lying or tapping into their imagination. When they look up to the left, they are remembering something by tapping into the memory of the brain. Vanessa Van Edwards, from the science of people, shares a simple formula that anyone can follow.

- Looking to their right is Auditory Thought (e.g., remembering a song).
- Looking to their left is visual Thought (e.g., remembering the color of a dress).
- Looking down to their right is someone creating a feeling or sensory memory (e.g., thinking what it would be like to swim in jello).
- Looking down to their left is someone talking to him or herself. [Source: scienceofpeople.com]

Mouth

Does the mouth also communicate important information? Yes, it does.

The mouth, especially the way the lips are positioned and used, can help us understand a lot about what someone else feels. There are numerous ways to squeeze the lips together, which creates a variety of communication signals. Although men and women use their lips to communicate non-verbally, you might realize most of the time that women will express far more with their mouths than men.

Lips are actually part of our skin. They are thin, sensitive, and packed with a lot of necessary nerve endings that make them very useful in our human interactions. If you noticed, other animals tend to have very different lips than ours. We seem to have extremely versatile and attractive lips, which is probably why they play a huge role in our sexual communication.

For example, when it comes to the emotional act of kissing, aren't you glad you've got lips that help you learn a lot about your partner just from a kiss? Unconsciously you can tell a lot from a kiss, and that's a key example of non-verbal communication. But whether you're kissing a lover or not, there are other cues you can look for when reading someone's mouth and lips. Some of these signals will come in very handy the next time you're engaged in conversation with a woman, as they tend to use many of these cues to communicate.

Perking the lips - This is usually a playful and cute gesture often communicated between lovers. Either to blow a kiss or to come across as flirtatious, so if you're planning on using it, make sure it's the right moment and the right person.

Pouting - This is when the lower lip slid forward and it is often used to indicate displeasure and insult.

Licking the lips - This can vary depending on the context, so make sure you understand what's happening to avoid misinterpretation. If it's a sexual lick, then it will be done intentionally and it begins in the corner of the mouth, licking the lower and upper lip in a slow sensual motion. It's indicative of desire. The other kind of lick is the nervous lick, which is quick and partial, often characteristic of tension. People who self-lick are often trying to release some pressure by self-soothing.

When you see someone biting their lip nervously, you can assume it means they are uncomfortable or uncertain about something. Unless, of course, they are trying to moisten their chapped lips or if it's a habit developed when they are in deep concentration.

Biting the lips - similar to licking it is also used to either communicate sexual desire, especially when a person wants to appear sexy. But it can also be a form of self-restraint, meaning the person is trying to contain anger or hold back thoughts.

The main thing to remember with all lip communication is that it is often indicative of sexual communication and tension control. We tend to either touch or use them for stimulation or self-comfort.

Breathing

How deep, shallow, quick, or slow the breath of a person is as they interact with you can tell you a lot about them. Breathing and emotions are connected, and a skillful person can easily read feelings through observing how another is breathing. Here are some signals to help you learn to determine what breathing patterns mean.

Heavy rapid breathing:

This might be an indication of fatigue and/or fear. When the heart beats faster, and the lungs need more oxygen, the breath becomes heavy and rapid. It feels like you need to catch your breath. Whenever you notice someone displaying that "catch your breath" type of scenario, it could be that they are tired from physical exertion, or they are terrified of something.

Deep breath:

That may be an indication of love or attraction and excitement, which is an intense positive emotion, or it could be anger and fear, which are also very intense on the negative side of the spectrum. Deep breathing is easy to notice if you're observant. If you give someone some news and they hold their breath or they take a deep breath in just before yelling out, that person is going to go through deep breathing patterns. On the other hand, we can spot this deep breathing when a guy wants to impress a girl. Before walking up to her, he might take a deep breath in to make his upper body look broader, and his abs look smaller, which is often attractive to the opposite sex.

Sigh:

Sighs generally communicate hopelessness, sadness, but sometimes they can be used to convey relief. If someone is waiting on a long struggle to end, they might sigh to express their sense of tiredness while hoping and praying for that relief to come.

ARMS, HANDS, AND FINGERS.

Now let's talk about different arm positions and what they might indicate.

The most basic and natural arms and hands gesture you will see is hands rested on the sides of the body.

Hands behind the back can be a signal of comfort and authority, or it can be the opposite i.e., tension and anxiety. How can you tell which is which? Observe for a while how the hands are wrapped around each other. If one hand is held easy in the palm of the other behind the back, that is more likely a superior position. In such a situation, the person would be seeking to use his body to demonstrate that he is secure and dominant in that particular context. Think of an army instructor or a professor on a podium. Suppose the person suddenly feels threatened by something or someone, they are more likely to shift into a tightly clenched grip to help them "keep it together" and if it becomes too much, they might change into a different position like folded arms.

Hands in the pockets tend to be received as something only people who are embarrassed or people who are hiding something (like the bad habit of fidgeting or nail biting) do.

LEGS AND FEET

Not many people pay attention to what the legs and feet are communicating in their own bodies as well as those of others. I mean, when was the last time you consciously monitored where your feet pointed as you engaged in conversation with another?

The reason we tend to neglect our legs and feet is that they are, in fact, furthest away from the brain, which prefers to focus on the face since that's the area of our body that's usually in the spotlight. But if you want to become great at reading people and their intention, paying closer attention to the legs and feet is a must. Take some time to notice what you do with your legs while you're standing as well as when you're sitting. What about the direction of your feet? Where do they point when having a business interaction? Does it change when you have a social or intimate interaction? How stable are you when standing?

Experts report there is a correlation between how a person stands and his or her self-confidence. For example, introverts will tend to stand with both feet very close to each other. This is usually a symbol of submission, and it makes the person a smaller target. It's easy to topple over someone standing like that both physically and socially. So if you're the kind of person who doesn't like drawing attention, it's likely your stance will be very narrow.

In contrast, if you're confident and want to come across as strong and dominating, your stance will be wider. When it comes to the direction of the feet, planting both feet directly in front of someone can come across as intimidating and hostile unless it's a person you're sexually attracted to, and you want to pass on that you're intimately interested in that person. For a more relaxed position, consider standing with your weight on one foot while the other points to the side. Now let's talk about some of the meanings you might derive when you spot different leg positions.

The stork is a very female gesture where she will stand on one foot while tucking the other behind her around the calf region (to form a stork). Females use this as a defense mechanism more than males mainly because men just lack that level of flexibility. It's so easy to destabilize such an individual, though, and perhaps above all else, when you notice this in a girl, be mindful of your approach because often this stance is communicating timidity and fear. Be gentle and attentive with your approach in the same way as you would a frightened animal.

Crossed legs, which is very common, doesn't necessarily mean the person is closed-minded. That's just a myth. It all depends on the context. For example, a person might want to pee. Or they might be relaxed in that environment in which case they are communicating that they are currently tied up and engaged in the ongoing interaction. The only time it can be a negative sign is where there's an outcome of suspicion, and the person is reserved and unwilling to change their mind. If they are just not convinced by you, they might cross their legs.

Happy feet are easy to spot and are often a result of feeling excited. If you want to tell a boy or girl who is walking on cloud nine, you just have to observe how "springy" their steps are. Happy people walk with jumpy strides; it's like they are about to lift off from the ground.

Chapter 12:
Face Expressions Analysis

Just like body language can say a lot about a person, so can facial expressions! Technically, facial expressions are an extension of body language. However, since there are so many of them it is always a good idea to look at this separately from other forms of body language. Let's look at what different facial expressions people are likely to have based on how they are feeling.

Anxiety

If a person is anxious, their eyes may dampen. They likely won't cry, but they may have a glisten to them. Their eyebrows will likely be tightly knit and their lower lip may tremble. You might notice a slightly wrinkled chin, as well as a tight mouth. Their face will likely be pointed downward as they try to avoid looking at what is making them anxious, or anyone else noticing how they're feeling.

Fear

Someone who is afraid will have their eyes wide and pointing downward. Their mouth will likely be opened, or they will be slightly frowning. Their eyebrows will be raised, and their chin will be pulled in.

You will also notice the color from their face disappears as they look pale, and their head will likely be pointing down.

Anger

If a person is angry, their eyes will widen. They will be staring at the subject of their anger, likely with their eyebrows pressed together toward the middle of their face. Their forehead will be wrinkled, and you may even see their nostrils flaring if they are angry enough. Their mouth will be tightly pursed or it may be open with tight lips as they show their clenched teeth. Usually, their chin will jut forward, and their face will start showing some red color.

Happiness

A happy and contented person usually smiles. They may have a wide-open smile, or a small and subtle smile depending on how happy they are at the moment. They are likely to laugh, and it's usually easier to make them laugh compared to people experiencing other emotions. Usually, they will get "crow's feet" on the sides of their eyes, and this is proof that they are genuinely smiling. Also, their eyes may look like they have a sparkle to them, and their eyebrows will be subtly raised. Their heads tend to be even on their neck and they are prone to look forward.

Sadness

Sad people tend to avoid eye contact. For this reason, they are often looking down. They may be crying, or their eyes may simply be tearful as if they are about to cry. Their lips will likely be pinched as they are trying to hold in the emotion, and their head will likely be down or turned away from the people around them.

Desire

When someone is experiencing the emotion of desire, their eyes widen and their pupils dilate. Their eyebrows are typically raised slightly, showing that they are interested in the person in front of them. Their lips will likely part slightly, or they may be puckered. They may even be smiling, depending on what is happening at the moment. Their head is usually tilted forward as though they are trying to get closer to that which they are feeling desirable for.

Interest

When someone is feeling interested in someone or something, they tend to have a very consistent gaze ahead of them. Their eyes may even squint as they show full attention to the subject of their interest. Their eyebrows will likely be subtly raised, further opening their expression. You may also notice they have their lips pressed together, and their head is pushed forward as they try and get closer to the subject of their interest.

Boredom

Bored people tend to look away with an expressionless face. They may appear as though they are not looking at anything in particular, and yet they are looking intently. This is because they are deep in thought, trying to remove themselves from the situation that is boring them. They may have a slight frown on their face. If they are especially bored, they may have their head resting on something such as their hand.

Surprise

Surprised people tend to have a very open expression. Their lips may be slightly parted, their eyebrows are raised, and their eyes are wide. Their head may even be tilted to the side or backward.

Disgust

People who are feeling disgusted often have their head turned away from what is causing their emotions to boil. They likely have flaring nostrils and their nose twisted up, with a tightly closed mouth. They may even push their tongue up against the back of their lips. Their chin is usually jutting forward.

Pity

When someone is feeling pity for someone else, they tend to have a very soft and sad look. Their eyes are typically soft and focused, and they may be damp. Also, their eyebrows might pull together slightly in the middle and their head will likely be turned to one side.

128

Chapter 13:
Tips and Tricks for Analyzing People

Regardless of whether at the workplace or out with companions, the non-verbal communication of the individuals around you says a lot. It has been proposed that non-verbal communication establishes over 60% of what we convey, so figuring out how to peruse the nonverbal signs individuals send is an important expertise. From eye conduct to the bearing in which an individual focuses their feet, non-verbal communication uncovers what an individual is truly thinking. The following are important hints to assist you with figuring out how to peruse non-verbal communication and better comprehend the individuals you connect with. Peruse the full article to gain proficiency with every one of the 8 basic non-verbal communication signals.

Concentrate on the Eyes

Eye conduct can be telling. When speaking with somebody, focus on whether the person in question looks or turns away. Failure to look can demonstrate weariness, lack of engagement, or even duplicity – particularly when somebody turns away and to the side. On the off chance that an individual looks down, then again, it regularly shows apprehension or accommodation. Likewise, check for widened understudies to decide whether somebody is reacting positively toward you. Students expand when subjective exertion increases, so if somebody is centered on a person or thing they like, their understudies will naturally widen. Understudy expansion can be hard to distinguish, yet under the correct conditions, you ought to have the option to spot it. An individual's flickering rate can likewise say a lot about what is happening inside. Flickering rate increases when individuals are thinking more or are focused. Now and again, expanded flickering rate shows lying – particularly when joined by contraction of the face (especially the mouth and eyes). Looking at something can propose a longing for that thing. For instance, if somebody looks at the entryway this may show a craving to leave. Looking at an individual can demonstrate a craving to converse with that person. With regards to eye conduct, it is likewise recommended that looking upwards and to one side during discussion shows a falsehood has been told while looking upwards and to one side demonstrates the individual is coming clean. The explanation behind this is individuals gaze upward and to one side when utilizing their creative mind to devise a story, and gaze upward and to one side when they are reviewing a genuine memory.

Look at the Face – Body Language Touching Mouth or Smiling

Although individuals are bound to control their outward appearance, you can in any case get on significant nonverbal signals on the off chance that you give close consideration. Consider the mouth when attempting to interpret nonverbal conduct. A straightforward grin nonverbal communication fascination system can be an amazing motion. Grinning is a significant nonverbal prompt to look for. There are various sorts of grins, including certifiable grins and phony grins. An authentic grin draws in the entire face, while a phony grin just utilizes the mouth. An authentic grin recommends that the individual is cheerful and appreciates the individuals around the person in question. A phony grin, then again, is intended to pass on delight or endorsement yet proposes that the smiler is feeling something different. A "half-grin" is another normal facial conduct that just draws in a single side of the mouth and shows mockery or vulnerability. You may likewise see a slight frown that keeps going exactly a second before somebody grins.

This commonly recommends the individual is concealing their disappointment behind a phony grin. Tight, pressed together lips additionally demonstrate dismay, while a casual mouth shows a casual frame of mind and positive state of mind. Covering the mouth or contacting the lips with the hands or fingers when talking might be a pointer of lying.

Focus on closeness

Closeness is the separation among you and the other individual. Focus on how close somebody stands or sits beside you to decide whether they see you positively. Standing or sitting in nearness to somebody is maybe probably the best marker of compatibility. Then again, on the off chance that somebody backs up or moves away when you move in nearer, this could be an indication that the association isn't shared. You can learn a great deal regarding the kind of relationship two individuals have by simply watching the closeness between them. Remember that a few societies lean toward less or more separation during cooperation, so closeness isn't a precise marker of closeness with somebody.

Check whether the other individual is reflecting you

Reflecting includes imitating the other individual's non-verbal communication. When cooperating with somebody, verify whether the individual mirrors your conduct. For instance, if you are sitting at a table with somebody and lay an elbow on the table, hold up 10 seconds to check whether the other individual does likewise. Another basic reflecting motion includes tasting a beverage. If somebody imitates your non-verbal communication, this is a generally excellent sign that the individual is attempting to set up compatibility with you. Have a go at changing your body stance and check whether the other individual changes theirs likewise.

Watch the head development

The speed at which an individual gestures their head when you are talking demonstrates their understanding – or absence of. Slow gesturing demonstrates that the individual is keen on what you are stating and needs you to keep talking. Quick gesturing demonstrates the individual has heard enough and needs you to complete the process of talking or give the person in question the go-ahead to talk. Tilting the head sideways during a discussion can be an indication of enthusiasm for what the other individual is stating. Tilting the head in reverse can be an indication of doubt or vulnerability. Individuals likewise point with the head or face at individuals they are keen on or share a partiality with. In gatherings, you can tell who the individual with the power is depending on how often other individuals take a gander at them as less important individuals are taken a gander at less frequently.

Take a gander at the other individual's feet

A part of the body where individuals frequently "release" significant nonverbal signals is the feet. The reason why individuals unexpectedly convey nonverbal messages through their feet is because they are generally so centered on controlling their outward appearances and chest area that significant hints are uncovered through the feet. When standing or sitting, an individual will for the most part point their feet toward the path they need to go. So, on the off chance that you see that somebody's feet are pointed toward you, this can be a decent sign that they have a positive assessment of you. This also applies to one-on-one conversations and gathering information about them. Indeed, you can deduce a ton of information just by contemplating the non-verbal communication cues from individuals involved, especially what direction their feet are pointing. Also, on the off chance that somebody seems, by all accounts, to be engaging in a discussion with you, but their feet are pointing towards another person, it is conceivable the individual would rather prefer to converse with that individual (except if the chest area proposes something else).

Watch for hand signals

Like the feet, the hands release significant nonverbal signals when looking at non-verbal communication. This is significant when perusing non-verbal communication so pay close attention to this next part. Watch non-verbal communication deliver pockets when standing. Search for specific hand signals, for example, the other individual placing their hands in their pockets or hand on head. This can show anything from anxiety to thorough misdirection. Oblivious pointing showed by hand motions can likewise say a lot. When making hand signals, an individual will point in the general bearing of the individual they share a liking with (this nonverbal prompt is particularly essential to look for during gatherings and when connecting in gatherings). Supporting the head with the hand by laying an elbow on the table can show that the individual is tuning in and is keeping the head still so as to stay concentrated. Supporting the head with the two elbows on the table can however, demonstrate weariness. At the point when an individual holds an item between the person in question and the individual they are interfacing with, this fills in as a boundary that is intended to shut out the other individual. For instance, if two individuals are talking and one individual holds a stack of paper before the person in question, this is viewed as a blocking demonstration in nonverbal correspondence.

Look at the situation of the arms

Think about an individual's arms as the entryway to the body and oneself. On the off chance that an individual folds their arms while associating with you, it is normally observed as a protective, blocking signal. Crossed arms can likewise show nervousness, weakness, or a shut personality. Whenever crossed arms are joined by a certified grin and by and large loosened up act, at that point, it can show a certain, casual disposition. At the point when somebody puts their hands on their hips, it is ordinarily used to apply some strength and is utilized by men more regularly than ladies.

Chapter 14:
How to Turn Manipulation Techniques to Your Advantage with NLP

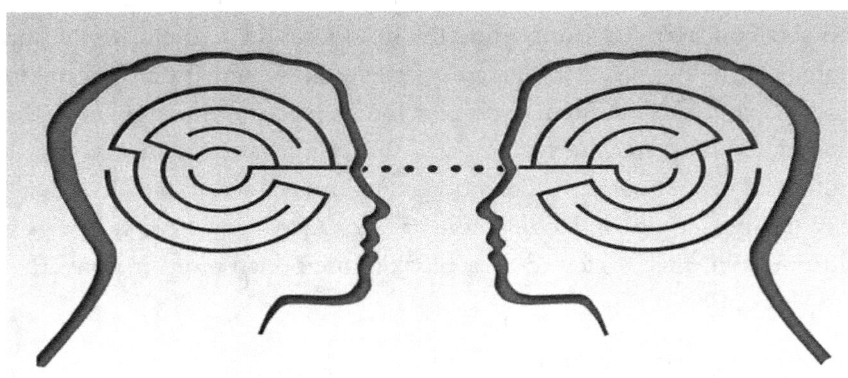

 Now you get to get into the bulk of the manipulation process! You are going to learn about the exact purpose of this book, and how you can master it. Since you have learned how to effectively analyze someone, it is time to learn how you can manipulate them effectively! Here you are going to understand what manipulation tactics exist, and which you should choose based on what drives your subject.

Manipulation is easy once you learn how, so take your time and focus on really mastering these steps so that you can rely on them in the future. It is also important that you do not skip to these steps before you have fully mastered how to analyze people. Manipulation will not be nearly as effective if you have not fully analyzed the person you are trying to manipulate, so you should take your time and master that part first. Then, mastering manipulation will become infinitely easier. You will likely find that it takes you minimal timing to really grasp the concept and make use of these tactics if you have already successfully analyzed your subject!

If you feel that you are ready, read on for the best-proven manipulation tactics out there!

Encourage Them to Say No

If you want to ask someone for something, such as for a sale or something big, you often want to start by asking something that you know they will say no to, first. You do this by encouraging the person to say no to you through a tactic such as asking for something outrageous or unreasonable first, then asking for what you actually want afterwards. You want to deliver it as somewhat of a two-part option, leading them to believe there is no third option. For example, you might say "So, would you like the four-year warranty for $999 or the six-year warranty for $1099?" Here, you did not ask if they wanted to go with no warranty at all. Instead, you gave them a choice to choose between a four-year and a six-year warranty. Since the six-year warranty is only an extra $100 and comes with two extra years of protection, this is the one you want to sell them. However, you need to get them to say yes, first. When you state it like this, you lead them to think about it. Then, you can add "Just so you know, the extra two years only cost $100 extra and it protects against everything from damage to natural breakdown. To me, it is a necessity to protect your investment." This way you have completely erased the idea of "no warranty" from their mind and made it a "necessity". You have also offered them an additional two years of protection for only $100. They are more likely to go with that option since it is more favorable to the shorter warranty for nearly the same cost.

By encouraging someone to say no to what you don't want, it makes it easier for you to get them to say yes to what you do want. Some other examples include things such as:

- "So, will that be a five-year contract or a two-year?"
- "Do you want to go on a date to the top of the Eiffel tower, or to the Keg tomorrow night?"
- "Would you rather stay here by yourself and wait with all of these strange people around, or come with me and keep me company while I run errands?"

By manipulating your phrasings to sound like the person only has two choices and both are ones you have picked for them, you ultimately get to decide which of the two the person is going to respond to. Since you have intentionally made one outrageous or unusual, or simply one that they would most likely say no to, they are more likely to say yes to the one you actually want them to agree with.

ESTABLISH SIMILARITY

People are attracted to people that they have similarities with. By creating the illusion that you have plenty in common with someone, you give the idea that you are the same. Through that, you are able to establish trust and chemistry. This will lead to the person liking you a lot more, even if they don't already know you. Once they feel this way toward you, they are far more likely to agree with you and want to do the things that you suggest. This is because they feel like you know them and that they can trust you to suggest things that would ultimately be to their benefit or favor. For example, you might say something like "I really like my TV, even though I paid $9,000 for it. It was expensive, but it was completely worth it. Because I love relaxing after work and enjoying the game while I eat dinner, it was a no brainer for me. I know that you like football too, and you have got to see what the game looks like on a TV with this resolution! It feels like you are really there, watching in real-time!" In this example, I am assuming that you have already established similarity and learned that your client is interested in football and enjoys having the best of the best. You also get the opportunity to overcome any money resistances that they may have toward the product. As you can see, similarity gives you "pull" with the person you are manipulating.

Establishing some similarity is easy. It comes from relating to what someone is saying and then sharing information that they would relate with as well. For example, if they say they like the color red, you would agree. Then later you would say something like "That is my favorite item, especially because it comes in the color red!" Here, you haven't directly stated that it comes in red for them. Instead, you have shared that you love red and it makes you excited. Since you already know they like red, they are more likely to feel as though they are similar to you because they would also be the type to get excited over this information. You can do this with virtually anything. If you are on a date, for example, you can express similarity by how you feel toward your career, your goals, and your life in general. You can share similarity by listening to what memories your date shares with you and sharing similar memories that you have, and ultimately by trying to create a situation where they feel like they understand you and you understand them, no matter how little you may know each other.

You can also use body language to establish similarity! This is more of a persuasion tactic, but it is still important in the manipulation process. The way master manipulators do this is through a practice called "pacing". That means that they essentially mirror a person's body language and use their cues, including verbal and non-verbal cues, to generate a feeling of similarity. Because you are behaving in a similar way to your subject, they feel as though you are similar to them on a deep, psychological level. They may not recognize it consciously, but their subconscious mind will recognize that you are copying them and it will take this as a sign that you and your subject share many similarities. You never want to be too obvious when doing this, but mirroring them to some degree is a great way to boost your morale with them and increase the pull you have when convincing them to do what you want them to do.

INSPIRE FEAR, THEN PROVIDE RELIEF

One very popular and highly effective way of manipulating people is to use fear. Whether someone is emotionally driven or logically driven, they are going to be easily moved and manipulated by fear. The trick with fear is to inspire fear in someone and then provide a solution for relief. This is a great tactic for selling stuff, spreading information (such as through the media), and for getting your way with virtually anything else.

This tactic works in an extremely simple two-step manner: cause the other person to fear something, and then give them a solution that inspires relief. In order to make the most of this tactic, you first want to have a general idea of what you can use to inspire fear. In other words, you will need to properly analyze the person so that you are clear on what they would actually be afraid of. Then, you can use this to create fear naturally. Once you have, you want the solution you are offering to be the form of relief.

Here is an example of inspiring fear and then offering relief:

News: "Today, sixteen people have died as a result of an attack by an unknown source. While many witnesses claim they know exactly who was responsible for the attack, authorities have not yet located the individual. In the meantime, twenty-three others are in the hospital to be treated for varying degrees of injuries, from minor scratches to extensive damage caused by the bullets spraying through the crowd. Stay tuned as we will provide you with updated information as the situation unfolds."

We are exposed to forms of manipulation, like the one above, daily. In very basic reality, we are fearful because many people were shot, and the attacker is still on the loose. Technically, the relief source would be the authorities who are actively searching for the attacker. However, the news broadcaster has shifted the relief to be the news station itself as they are claiming to be the ones that will provide us with live updates and who will inform us when the attacker is finally caught. Therefore, instead of relying on the authorities for relief from the fear, the audience is relying on that news broadcaster.

The ultimate goal is to make your product, service, offer, or solution one that provides relief from a real fear. When people are afraid, they are often desperate for a solution that will alleviate the fear and make them feel safe and comfortable once more. If you are the one who can invoke the fear (without making it look intentional) and then provide relief (without making it look staged), then you are the one who orchestrates both parts of the strategy. This means that you can easily "sell" your solution because the person you are talking to is actively "buying".

USE GUILT, PLAY THE VICTIM

For people who are driven by emotion, manipulating feelings of guilt and playing the victim are two great ways to manipulate people. These ways tend to be more obvious if you are not careful, but if you plan it properly you can use these without seeming like you are intentionally manipulating the other person. Instead, they will see that you "need" their assistance and they will be eager to provide it.

Using guilt means that you essentially guilt someone into doing what you are asking of them. There are many ways that guilt can be manipulated, depending on the situation at hand. For example:

- "But you owe me, remember when I helped you?"
- "You don't want to disappoint me on my birthday again, do you?"
- "I recall you told me last time you purchased her a gift it was not what she wanted. You wouldn't want to be responsible for two bad gifts, would you?"
- "I covered your shift last week and you can't help me cover mine now?"
- "I run all of the errands that you ask of me, why are you going to try and make me do this one, too?"

By using guilt, you can make people feel as though they are obligated to comply or agree with you. Because you can point out a genuine reason as to why they "owe" you, they feel as though they have to fulfill that obligation. People do not like to feel indebted, and using guilt is a great way to make them feel as though they have to help you or do what you have asked. This is how they can make sure that they don't "mess up again", or "take advantage" after all!

Playing the victim works synonymously with using guilt to get your way. Playing the victim essentially means that you make people feel as though they are asking unreasonable things from you. As a result, they are more likely to comply and give in to what you want from them because they feel guilty that they were the ones "trying to manipulate you", even though technically you are manipulating them with this tactic! It works like this:

- "I can't believe you would ask that of me! After all, I've done for you? Why would you take advantage of me like this?"
- "I have never once treated you the way you are treating me now, what makes you think that is okay? I don't deserve this."
- "I was only doing what you asked of me, it's not my fault you didn't ask clearly!"
- "What, am I not good enough to do ______ for you?"
- "Do you really think of me like that? What did I do to make you think so lowly of me?"

When you switch into the victim card, people automatically feel as though they have been unkind to you. Then, they turn into a mode where they want to "fix" the situation. That is where you get to offer them your solution. Because they want to make you feel better, they are far more likely to say yes so that you won't be so upset anymore. As a result, you get your way!

USE LOGIC TO APPEAL TO RATIONAL PEOPLE

People who are logically-driven are also emotionally-driven, as you know, but they also require you to cater to their logical side if you are going to actually get anywhere with them. This is not as hard as it sounds, but it does take some practice.

Using logic to appeal to rational people mostly works through providing a lot of factual evidence and statistics that back up what you are trying to "sell" or "solve". This can work in many different ways, but ultimately you want to infuse as many facts as you can. You want to make it seem as though you know all of the facts that are required for someone to decide so that they don't go and look for the facts themselves. For example, say you want to sell something to someone. Perhaps it is a skincare product that was created to help people with dry skin. The facts in the following statement are not accurate, but they will provide you with an idea of what the "solution" should sound like:

"You mentioned you have a problem with dry skin, right? I have this incredible skincare solution for you. Did you know approximately 60% of the population has moderate to severe issues with dry skin? This cream was tried on a group of 100 people and 99 of them claimed it made their skin feel smoother in as little as three days. Within a week, their dry skin symptoms had completely disappeared and they were back to feeling comfortable and confident in their own skin! It is made using a special ingredient that we have created in our own labs. It is a patented technology that was designed to help cater specifically to problematic dry skin. It gets deep into the pore and infuses it with moisture, essentially hydrating it. Imagine taking a big drink of water when you are really thirsty! That is what it is like for your pores when you use this skincare product. Would you like to try some on? (Apply the lotion to their dry skin now.) It is only $39.99 for a bottle, but today we are giving away two bottles for the price of one! So, if you buy one you get one completely free! Are you interested?"

Here, you took the time to fully educate the person on how the product works. You incorporated a large number of facts, statistics, and explanations as to how the product works. Rather than solely targeting the emotional side of their problem (for example, a lowered sense of self-esteem from problematic dry skin), you appealed to the logical side of them, too. However, you were not completely focused on logic. You did include words like "comfortable" and "confident" to appeal to the underlying emotional side that they have which would also need to be appealed to in order to successfully manipulate a logically-driven person.

By tailoring your solution to feature many facts, evidence, and statistics, you make it so that those with logical minds are more likely to want to purchase the product you are selling, agree to help you in some way, or otherwise engage in your solution or pitch. As a general rule of thumb, if you are uncertain as to whether or not someone is logically-driven, it is helpful to include a few facts in your pitch. Appeal equally to both sides and gauge their response to see how they react. If they seem to emphasize on the facts you have shared, share more. If they are more interested in the emotional benefits, elaborate on those. Paying attention to their reaction is a great way to continue to appeal to what they need to hear for them to agree with you and do whatever you have asked or take what you have offered.

BRIBE THEM

Bribery is a phenomenal tool. It works on getting children to complete their chores, and it works on adults when you need it to as well. You can easily use bribery in many different situations to help get what you want. In some cases, bribery will be obvious. In others, it may not be quite so obvious. You will want to choose how obvious you make it depending on the situation. For example, if you are trying to use guilt and bribery together to get your friend to loan you their car for the weekend, you might say something like "Come on, don't you remember all of the times I helped you? Don't you owe it to me? If you help me out this once I promise to take you out to your favorite restaurant on Monday, completely on me!" Wording something like this will make it very clear that you are trying to bribe the person you are talking to. There are many instances where this type of thing works, but many where it won't, also. In general, this is a better solution to use in personal relationships where you know the person and you know what you can and cannot get away with.

If you need to hide your bribery, you can word your sentence differently. For example, say you are trying to sell an expensive product to someone. You start by putting the product in their hands and getting them to interact with it. Then, once they comment something to do with them liking the product, you say something like: "Yeah, that is a phenomenal product! Plus, we have an amazing promotion going on right now where if you purchase that product you get a free (other product) with it! It's an incredible deal, and a great way to try out a couple of new things to see what you like the most, without spending more money!" Here, you look like you are simply offering greater value, and not trying to bribe the person into buying the product.

Chapter 15:
Using Body Language for Persuasion and Mind Control

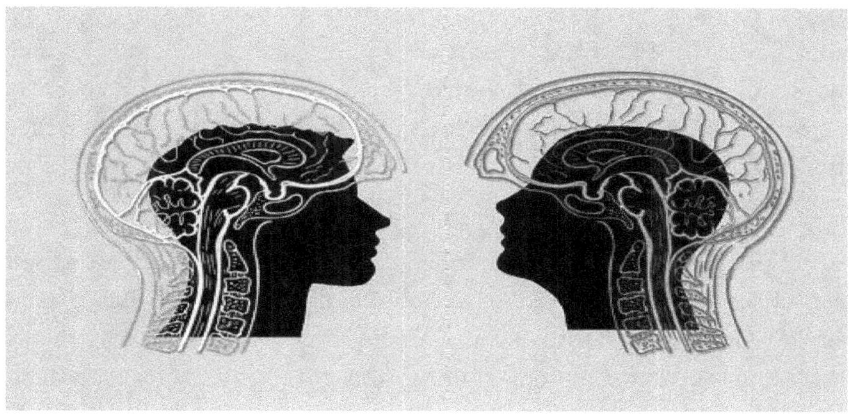

Know that actions speak louder than words, so being aware of the impact that body language can have is important. With the use of non-verbal communication, you can influence the way that other people think, perceive, and act. It is a powerful concept that you can master. Being great with body language means that you not only have to use it effectively, but you also must be aware of the cues that are used by other people. If you can utilize this skill, then your positive manipulation efforts will almost always be successful.

SMILE GENUINELY

A smile can change the entire mood of a conversation. When you are talking to someone, simply flashing a smile can make a difference between the other person deeming you trustworthy or not. The great thing about smiling as a social cue is that it signifies many different things. It can mean that you are in agreement with or understand what the other person is saying. Without verbally saying anything in return, you can put someone at ease. This is a great tool for appearing to be accepting and inviting. This is one way you can use to control someone's mind by getting to this point of acceptance. Remember this during any manipulation methods that you try.

If a person is trying to humor you, smiling can show them that you find them amusing. This is a confidence booster, and it becomes especially helpful when you are trying to become close to someone. This action shows that you are friendly and approachable. Always share genuine smiles with other people because some are great at noticing the fake ones. When you smile, you should mean it. Any fake action that you take will only make the other person question your intentions when they find out about it. Plus, you will also feel better knowing that you can be your true self.

The same way that smiling at others can enhance a conversation, you can also pay attention to the amount of time that the other person smiles. Non-verbal communication is important because it says things that words sometimes can't. You will know exactly how to proceed with your positive manipulation when you know where you stand with another person. Reading body language leaves no room for guesswork; it can be hard when you have to fill in the blanks about how someone is feeling.

Working on your smile is important if you want to appear charismatic. It is with this type of charisma that you become great at positive manipulation. This, combined with the ability to read other people, will provide you with a well-rounded sense of moods and emotions. It is normally difficult for people to hide a smile, so this is why it is often a good indicator of exactly what is going on in their mind. Not only is this a great social tool, but it will also make you feel good. The more you smile, the happier you will feel.

CASUAL TOUCH

Touch can become a big part of social interaction once you become comfortable with it. There are definite boundaries between comfortable, casual touches and those that are shared only within intimate relationships. Generally, quick arm and shoulder touches are deemed appropriate when you are positively manipulating someone. This adds a sense of closeness to the conversation, even if you are not particularly close with the person just yet. Utilizing casual touch states that you understand or that you can relate. It makes you appear to be approachable, much like smiling can.

There are simple ways that you can add casual touching into your conversational skills. One of the easiest is to touch the person's arm when you are expressing words of emphasis. This will draw the other person into what you are saying. You can also incorporate touching when a deep topic is being covered. For example, if your friend expresses that she just lost her job, a casual touch would be appropriate as you express your sympathies. Using this method will give you control over the conversation. When you touch someone, you are the one who is directing the energy.

The touching must be kept on a strictly casual basis. One of the worst ways you can betray someone's trust is by breaking this simple boundary. Remember, you want to show that you are respectful while also remaining approachable. A mistake that is often made is utilizing casual touching too much. Even if no boundaries are broken, it can become awkward when it is happening in excess. When you are first starting out, try only using it to emphasize certain things that you say. There is no need to overdo it.

As with any form of non-verbal communication, you can also judge a person's comfort level by how much they utilize casual touching. Arms crossed and distance being kept will normally signify that you have some more work to be done before you can attempt to control that person. This closed-off body language likely means that you are not to be trusted. An open stance with some casual touching is a great sign; this means that the other person is comfortable with you. If you get these signals, you are likely ready to positively manipulate a situation involving this person. Sometimes, people utilize casual touching when they are nervous. If their gaze is flighty, yet casual touching is still happening you might need to wait for a clearer signal that the person is truly comfortable with you.

FIRM AND GENTLE HANDSHAKE

Your handshake says a lot about your personality type. Whether you are in a professional setting or meeting a mutual friend for the first time, your handshake is the first impression. When you are in this position, you will want to remember to come across as friendly yet respectable. This balance can be tough to accomplish when you do not have an accurate handshake to match. Put some thought into the type of message that you send to other people when you first meet them. Do you have a firm grip? Do you maintain eye contact? Is there a smile on your face? All these things matter very much when it comes to your handshake.

The key to having a good handshake is having multiple different ones for different occasions. If you are in a professional setting, the handshake will naturally be firmer than a handshake you would give to a friend in a bar. The firmness of your handshake indicates the level of dominance that you are trying to portray during the interaction. Of course, positively manipulation does require dominant energy. You need to be the one who can change things by way of simple suggestions. If you do not maintain this role right away, you will have a lot more work to do later on.

Being firm does not have to be rough. You don't want to hurt the other person with your handshake. Keep the pressure at a reasonable level. Think about how you would like them to shake your own hand. There is no need to overdo the grip when you also have several other body language cues that you can utilize. The handshake is merely meant to provide you with a solid starting point, and then the rest can follow. When you get into the habit of shaking hands with other people, it may feel formal at first, but you must know how to channel your energy into getting what you want.

Eye contact plays a role in your handshake, as well. The amount of eye contact that you hold can convey different messages to the other person. Not enough of it suggests that you are bluffing or weak. A person might question your motives if you appear to be distracted in this way. Too much of it can be mistaken as a challenge, which you don't want. Starting conflict is not the best way to lead to positive manipulation. You should maintain enough eye contact to remain confident, but not too much that you start making others feel uncomfortable.

THE POWER OF CORRECT POSTURE: MIRRORING THEIR POSTURE

You are probably familiar with the idea that you receive the energy that you give. This is something to pay attention to when you are talking to people. Your posture is the way that you present yourself to the world. Having slumped shoulders can signify disappointment, sadness or even apathy. Keeping them pushed back with your chin up can exude confidence and pride. The way that you decide to stand is very important to every single social interaction that you have. There is no way for you to win someone over by appearing closed off or unapproachable. Some people will follow all the correct steps of positive manipulation but forget to correct their posture. The right posture can make all the difference.

If you are unsure about how you should present yourself to someone, simply mirror their posture. This is usually the best way to gauge your role in the given situation. If someone is being open with you, keeping their stance forward using their hands to explain things, try doing the same. When someone feels that you are on the same page as them, it becomes much easier to converse. For those who are colder to start with, try to reel back your enthusiasm. It can be overwhelming when one person is clearly expressing that it will take some time to become comfortable, and the other person continues to push boundaries. Your best bet is to remain as neutral as you can until the other person does something otherwise.

When you mirror a person's posture, don't make it obvious. Of course, you do not want to copy their exact mannerisms. This becomes insulting or comical if you are caught imitating. You can still be on the same page without doing the same thing. For instance, if your boss is angry, your endless banter and casual touching won't make the best impression. Each situation will be different, so you must use your common sense. It is best to accept anger and disappointment exactly as they are presented to you. Keep a strong physical stance but remain facing the person. By turning away, this suggests that you are closed off or do not care about what is being explained to you.

When someone is ready to express happiness, they will stand a lot closer to you. They might even smile a lot and partake in casual touching. When you experience this, you know that you can also relax a bit more during the interaction. As you match the behaviors, the demeanor also becomes synchronized. It is impossible to do this with someone who cannot empathize. It takes a truly empathetic person to be able to mirror any type of posture, good or bad.

Eye Contact

Eye contact is an extremely relevant form of non-verbal communication. The eyes hold plenty of valuable information behind them. A simple furrow of the brow can reveal true feelings in an instant. It is thought that maintaining eye contact with someone makes you a more trustworthy person. Being able to look into someone's eyes without wavering suggests that you are being genuine. For whatever reason, eye contact can be hard for a lot of people. Even if you value your honesty and integrity, maintaining eye contact with someone during a conversation can take some practice.

We tend to shy away from eye contact because it can make us feel vulnerable. While you do not need to completely drop your guard around those you make eye contact with, you do need to make sure that you trust them to the best of your own ability. This mutual reciprocation will give you the certainty that you can make a positive influence in this person's life. It shows that the interaction goes beyond any surface-level small talk that normally occurs. Just as keeping eye contact can be hard; it might also be hard to interact with someone who gives it too intensely. It almost becomes a personal challenge to see who can maintain it the strongest and for the longest.

It is best to not engage in these kinds of challenging behaviors. Remember, you must be in control of how the situation flows. Keep things as positive as you can but know that you should ultimately be the one who is guiding the way that everything unfolds. You will want to place yourself in a position of power without the other person fully realizing it. This is what gives you the upper hand with positive manipulation. Be aware of the eye contact that you do maintain in your daily life and think about ways that you can improve it. Do you need to do it more often? Could you do without some of it? Are you making people feel the way that you need them to feel? All of these questions must be taken into consideration.

You will find that eye contact is one of the most powerful forms of body language that exists. It can hold so much expression behind it because of the way that our eyes seem to tell silent stories. When a person is experiencing pain or hardship, you will likely be able to see it in their gaze before they express this to you. These are things that you need to look out for. You should always aim to be one step ahead of what the other person is thinking or feeling, coming up with valuable solutions that can be implemented

Conclusion

In this book, we've covered everything important for avoiding manipulation and encouraging positive persuasions in how to interact with others. It is not something you can achieve overnight, but with more practice, you can remember that you have what you need to get what you want the most. The major mistake you make after learning these methods is to use them favorably and keep them away from others, rather than spreading the happiness and satisfaction gained through the influence. It is easier to spread negativity than persuading positively. Persuasion sometimes means building trust. Manipulation simply means increasing fear. It may be easier to operate, but in the end, it will be much harder to clean up.

Remember that this process begins with really understanding the character of a person. There are common types of manipulators, and this personality trait may be immediately felt by someone else. Similarly, you can see that there are hidden properties that are not always visible first. Keep in mind that not all human manipulation behaviors are symbolic of a malicious person. Parental operations and long-term partners can say or do things that you can do in this way, even though they are not intended to do so because they can interfere with our behavior. Always pay attention to your intent when deciding whether someone can really operate. Also, keep in mind that body language can play a big role in how someone is perceived. If you notice what this type of body language looks like, you can see a body language that is more compelling to others than before. Make sure you know your body language and that others are not manipulating it.

Ultimately, manipulation is generally a way to get what people want most. We all have basic human needs and instincts that determine our behavior. If we are not careful about how we get these things, we can hurt others. The more skills we have to make a positive impact, the easier it is for us to meet our deepest desires healthily and for the benefit of many. Remember that it starts with a small moment of persuasion to increase your influence. Do not tell people what to do. But encourage them from the personal experiences and stories they have learned from others. Do not try to let someone do something you do not want. Be honest with rewards and consistency so that you can make the right decisions for yourself.

Always think about your actions to make sure you are doing the right thing. Some trust is associated with influence. If you are not careful, you are hooked on the feeling that this trust goes far beyond anyone else and feels best for everyone. The more you can reflect your thoughts and make sure you have the right intentions, the more legitimate you are. Doing the right thing can be difficult when the simplest is most beneficial to you, but keep in mind that you are sensitive to others. It can be difficult, but if you do it in a fair and rewarding way, you will eventually get what you want most.